Mary Magdalene

The Christos~Sophia Revelation

Volume 1

Jewels Maloney

Mary Magdalene: The Christos-Sophia Revelation

Dancing with The Sun Productions

2nd Edition November 2012

1st Edition July 2012

ISBN-13: 978-0-9790871-4-1
ISBN-10: 0-9790871-4-7

jewelsmaloney@gmail.com

Cover artwork courtesy of Children of the Sun Humanitarian Foundation
www.childrenofthesun.org

Symbolic of the vibrational pattern of Ascended Master Saint Germaine

Artist: Erial Ali
erial.ali@gmail.com

Interior Photographs

Jewels Maloney

Bless you Daisy and
all the Love & Light
you Bring to our
Beautiful Planet!
xo's Jewel

Dedicated to All That Is

and to All of Us

as One Family

of Mother Earth

Other titles by Jewels Maloney

Every Child is Holy

Ecstasies and Meditations - Poetry & Channeling

Wadogh - I Am Thankful -Poetry

Books and Photographs available at

www.AscensionIsNow.com

Table of Contents

Sun Rise, Boynton Canyon
Sedona, AZ

Chapter 1.

Introduction

As we all entered into the 21st century on Mother Earth, the voice of The Magdalene began to be heard in story, film, sacred texts, oral traditions that were finally being written down and disseminated, and from people connecting with The Magdalene energies and channeling her messages of love, truth and wisdom. Many women and men have felt the call of The Magdalene in their hearts, and have joined in this great journey of birthing and demonstrating the Feminine and the Masculine Christ Consciousness, which brings into fruition a new wholeness, unity, unconditional love and creative joy. This has been called The Sacred Marriage, and it is an inner union that will then also be reflected in outer relationships. All relationships then become ones of equality and unity. This is a state of consciousness called love!

Why is The Magdalene's voice now being heard? Because we are in a new cycle of the planetary, galactic, universal and cosmic story - a cycle which will be characterized and expressed as unity and oneness, equality and freedom, and the nurturing, creative, healing, joyful power of love. The story of The Magdalene brings forth the Divine Feminine aspect of Creator. Magdalene points us to Mother God - the Goddess - the Sophia, and brings us all into wholeness. The Magdalene and Sophia and all they represent have been denied and suppressed and hidden for not only centuries, but millennia - and all of the qualities of the divine feminine that dwell in all of us, were trampled underfoot and shoved into darkness as the fear based need to control and dominate; and imbalanced ego concerns of pride, power, and greed gained ascendancy in the human experience and psyche and spread to all aspects of society and life until the entire planet and all her creatures almost suffocated and became extinguished. But the destruction of Mother Earth and all her life, and the destruction of humanity and all it's truth and beauty could not and would not become extinct. Humanity loves stories of heroism and heroines.

Humanity loves happy endings. There is a reason for this! This was our destined role: humanity was to live through vast inner and outer darkness and come out in the end understanding, feeling, and knowing the truth of who we are: Love. And thus, Love and self-realization would ultimately prevail and humanity would "win the day".

The forces of light and love throughout creation, near and far, came to assist us in our heroic destiny and in a miraculous and very eventful birthing - a birth that has great meaning to all civilizations and sentient beings throughout this universe and beyond, as we all journey in to the Heart of Mother-Father God. The whole truth is being told. What has been suppressed is arising. We are realizing who we truly are, have always been, and will always be. We are each a trinity of wholeness - divine masculine, divine feminine and divine child within. We are eternal beings, ever creating, co-creating, and re-creating in an astonishing array of life forms and energy streams.

Mary said, "I will teach you what is hidden from you." The Gospel of Mary

"She spoke these words as a woman who understood all things." The Dialogue of the Savior

"When Mary had said these things, she turned their hearts toward the good." The Gospel of Mary

Chapter 2

The Christos-Sophia Revelation Planet Earth 2012

"I am the mind of she who seeks, and the rest of those who sojourn. I am the understanding of my question, and the one who is found by those who seek. I am the answer of those who ask of me. I am the power of all powers in my knowledge, and of angels who have been sent forth by my command. And of gods in their time by my wisdom, and the spirit of all those who exist within me. And of those who dwell within me."

~ The Thunder, Perfect Mind

The Nag Hammadi Scrolls

2012 is the time for the Reappearance of The Christ, and for what the Gnostic traditions call The Reception of The Bride. This is the time when The Magdalene is seen and known as the One with The Christ: the time when the Divine Feminine, often called Sophia is recognized as the Beloved of Creator and the birther of all manifested creation. The Divine Masculine cauldron of Light - the spark, the fire of creative intelligence as One with the Divine Feminine cauldron of Love and creative intelligence unite, interplay, and love forever. And creation evolves, expands, and perfects itself forever.

This time is the marker of the culmination of a Divine Plan for humanity and Gaia as we enter into the 7th Golden Age on Mother Gaia. Our collective ascension, which means rising in consciousness and vibration or frequency, enlightening on all levels of our being, and living from the heart will affect our Galaxy, all the Galaxies of this Universe, and All That Is. The full merging of the Divine Masculine and Feminine Creator with the human creation in all its glory is succeeding and this heroic journey will bring great color and brightness to all of creation. It will bring all that is the glory of being human - deep feelings, wondrous perceptions, great thoughts and revelations, great works of creativity, and wonderful circles of connection and love in to full blossoming over the coming centuries and millenia. This is happening now. The foundation has been well laid.

Beloved Mother Earth is a focal point at this cosmic time of the in breath of God when All That My Father and My Mother Have and Are is to be given and shared as One with the fullness of human consciousness, feelings and physical form. This dispensation is being spoken, heard and felt through many voices and many hearts, as it is the truth encoded into every heart without fail. It is spoken in every language as well as in the telepathic rapport of every soul with All That Is. It is spoken in many worlds throughout the infinite galaxies and universes. It is the law of the Omniverse resounding throughout creation.

The Christos-Sophia is here now, physically embodied in many forms - female and male. We are androgynous, which is the truth of all forms in the higher realms of light, and also the truth of every human being, who is now experiencing the "marriage" of the human and the divine, and of the inner divine masculine and divine feminine. The marriage of the divine eternal I AM Presence with the magnificence of the human being creates Self-realized, God-realized, fully sovereign cosmic beings of love, light, and power. This power is creativity utilizing the energies of love and light, to explore and embody in infinite creations. The marriage of the inner divine masculine and feminine gives birth to the divine child within - the authentic, free, creative human spirit that is and always has been, love.

The flowering of seeds planted eons ago, when the Heart of All That Is - the Divine feminine life force, joined with the Divine masculine fire of illumination and intelligence is now celebrating the union and unity which will bring forth unprecedented creativity, joy, harmony and celebration in all worlds. Springtime has come to the micro and macrocosms, and the joyous celebration of unity, love, and peace is resounding back and forth across the cosmos from the heart of All That Is. For humanity, what this means is the full merge of the Divine Eternal I AM Presence with the divine structures of the human as a creation of love and perfection. Each chakra of the human design and all energy fields of the human experience, are beautiful and varied ways to receive and express Spirit - the Cosmic Fire of Love, Wisdom, Compassion, and Creativity flowing through the dance of chakric expressions in infinite subtleties of creative purpose and play. From the root chakra of fulfillment, security and connection with Mother Earth through the crown chakra and our connection with Our Source, we are a rainbow of expression, creating a rainbow bridge to more expanded versions of ourselves in the flowering of a grand experiment which is now coming to fruition in this time - what the Cherokee so beautifully call the Age of Flowers.

The breaking apart of the old world and of the past structures, institutions, belief systems and limiting boxes which no longer serve the grandness of your spirit within, has ultimately served to unveil the heart of humanity which in truth is unselfish and is pure love, passion, and play.

Archway of Apples, Chalice Well Gardens

Glastonbury, England

Chapter 3

From Jewels

I have been asked to tell my personal story. It began with my birth on February 19th, 1955 to a family full of great love. I was born at 0 degrees 33 minutes of Pisces on the cusp of Aquarius, with Virgo rising.

In my 22nd year, January of 1977, I experienced an At-One-Ment with All That Is. In an unexpected flash of cosmic consciousness, I realized that I AM and Everything Is God/dess, that there is no death, that we are eternal beings of love, and that all of Creation is pulsing in Oneness. After the initial bliss and expansion of consciousness, I was catapulted into my first "dark night of the soul" when I met what esoteric traditions call "The Dweller on the Threshold". The Dweller is all the shadow aspects of ourselves over which our ego stands guard. The ego keeps us pre-occupied with mental chatter and the belief that all the answers are in the outer world, and that it has everything under control.

When a huge spiritual opening occurs, it opens the doors to our unconscious material, our own personal akashic record of our entire soul's journey that we hold in our cellular memory, DNA, and energy fields. The veils between the dimensions drop away, and much more is seen and felt and known. This experience of cosmic consciousness also triggers what I later came to call "The Christing Initiation" which is when the heart bursts open and the true journey of spiritual mastery begins. When this happens, we begin to be taught from within. Our soul or Higher Self begins to receive and respond to the telepathic teachings of higher forces of love, light, and wisdom. These teachings are revealed in both the interface with our relationships, work, travel, study, and all areas of human living as well as from an inner unfolding revelation of truth which ultimately leads to inner peace, great love, and wisdom. We begin to learn on what is called "the inner planes" from the Ascended Master guides who have tread that path before us, and from our teams or councils of guides, guardians, and ancestors of the light, and from our own I AM Presence and direct connection to God/dess or All That Is. Higher mind abilities also open. For me, I began to automatically translate everything into numerology. I could see and know what the dark forces on this planet were doing to suppress the spirit of humanity. And I could read symbolism in everything around me.

The path of spiritual mastery has many steps and we must master each one. Some of these steps are unconditional love for everyone and everything - seeing Great Spirit alive in everything and feeling how alive everything in creation is, and opening the heart more and more until it encompasses All That Is. We also master humility - learning from everyone and thus growing in the recognition of The Divine. Service to others and to Mother Earth as the central focus of one's activity in the world are just a few of the steps we take along our path of rising in consciousness and vibration. As we move along, we become liberated from the past, from karma, from programming and conditioning; and we become every more absorbed in The Oneness of All That Is, living ever more in an inner stillness and peace. This does not preclude joy, fun, laughter, creativity, and celebration of all kinds but rather enhances all of these qualities of being fully alive.

My life has had many chapters and I explored many things. I learned from children as a day care teacher, participated in disarmament efforts and with a group called Food Not Bombs. I was part of a band called Jai, and various multi-media theater groups in Boston, MA. I received a Masters and doctorate in creativity and was a professor of teachers. I co-created and founded two nature-based schools for children - one in Montana and one in Northern California. My life has been full and rich with many people and travels and living in many different places on this beautiful planet including northern New York, western Massachusetts, the mountains of Montana, northern California, Sedona, and Oxford, England.

When I first moved to Sedona, Arizona in June of 2001, I was impressed by the number of people channeling higher energies, wisdom, and healing in this beautiful and magnificent sacred site of our beautiful planet. I sat myself down beside a beautiful turquoise pool surrounded by bamboo saying to myself that I could channel too. What came through was a poem from The Magdalene. This was the beginning of a more conscious connection with The Magdalene for me personally, a merging of consciousness, and will be the place we will now begin...

Magenta Berries, Killarney

Co. Kerry, Ireland

Chapter 4

From Mary Magdalene

Spirit of breath on the soft wind

Speaks gently to the Heart of Humanity.

Sun reflects aquamarine, cobalt and emerald waves

Rippling over the mighty ash tree,

Reflecting the effervescent Beauty of Light.

This Beauty resides in the Hearts and Souls of Humanity.

Clear, rippling out to all the Universes,

Calling all our companions to enter in

To Gaia's fields of joy and to sparkle.

You have emerged from the Void,

Co-creating this day of sparkling Joy

On a planet pregnant with Love, Light, and Power.

This light is bursting forth in waves of love,

Felt in the deepest Central Suns,

Celebrated by angels, fairies,

Mermaids, mermen and dolphins,

our star sisters and brothers.

All the Kingdoms and Queendoms of Earth

And the Source of All That Is.

All resonate in cosmic harmonies with Joy.

Allow your frequencies of joy and love, peace and bliss to penetrate deeply the fears you attempt to hold in the shadows.

Let go, into your great choruses of devotion and celebration, your appreciation and regard for All That Is.

Bring your gifts of this day to the Source.

Drink deep and return with a golden platter

for the feasting of the thousands of souls who dance

in your entourage.

Wear the golden crown graciously.

We are All crowned together -

a vast spiral of sister and brotherhood, dancing lightly -

emanating sparkling star light - fire!

God-sparks, we dance with our sister Gaia

and all her millions and millions of crowned jewels.

Dance! In the radiance of the life and love of the soul.

~ June 2001

From Ecstasies and Mediations - Poetry and Channeling.

Light Being

in the Double Spiral of the Goddess Crop Circle

near Avebury, England July 2010

Chapter 5

Trust

Greetings Beloved Ones, I AM the Magdalene and I Come Forth from the Heart of Our Creator, and from the Void of the Great Mother where all potential for Creation swims in great Joy.

I AM asking you to *trust* Creator and the intricate and benevolent weave of Creation – a weave so delicate and so precise that to see and feel it in the events and relationships and awakenings of your Life brings the utmost awe and reverence for Creator, Creation, for yourself and for All That Is.

I AM asking you to Trust this Creation, the Divine Feminine out of which All Is Born – Ever New and Ever Eternal. The Great Divine Feminine is the rich and abundant womb of All That Is ever manifesting the heart's desires throughout All the Universes.

But most important, I AM asking you to trust yourself, to honor yourself, to love *all* of yourself: your darkness and your light, and all the tones of colors in all the spectrums so that you can and will be *free* – a Sovereign Universal Being of love-light and creative power, empowered to re-create on your planet *now*.

You have all been disempowered. The ways of disempowerment have been myriad and long-standing and are lodged in your subconscious mind. You have all lost trust in yourselves, your own divine inner teacher, and your true nature, which is love. This truth in your heart has been covered over through the old paradigm institutions, belief systems, and emotional wounding that went before you and were then passed on to you. The four pillars of the old paradigm that is now dissolving in to the past were victim consciousness, poverty consciousness, lust consciousness, and conditional love consciousness.

When a soul does not feel love on this earth plane, a great emptiness and longing is ever-present and this longing tries to find and fill the emptiness that is felt. There are few of humanity who have been born and grown and unfolded feeling truly loved and thus loving themselves and trusting others and their world.

It is time now to re -claim yourself, the truth of who you are. You are a Divine Eternal Being of love and creativity, of peace and of passion, a Being who not only knows, but *is* the truth. The moment you recognize from deep within that you are all of this, you will bring rorth through your own Being and your experiences the four pillars of the New Earth, the essential qualities of the Aquarian Age: Victory consciousness, Abundance consciousness, Divine Unconditional Love consciousness, and Unity consciousness.

And then, you will find yourself trusting your self and all others, no matter who they are, what they look like, how old they are, how different they are from you. You will find yourself trusting that All That Is: both

Divine Creator and Divine Creation, is in every particle and sub-atomic particle and all the "space between". There is no-where God/dess, Goodness is not. Every particle of creation is filled with the original and divine energy. Every particle of life everywhere is inter-connected in the vast ocean of life. It is only a matter of dropping every veil, every mask, and every fear you have taken upon yourself to walk naked in your Divinity; innocent, childlike, all-encompassing, all-embracing wisdom and truth. And you can do this simply by saying YES! Yes! I Know Who I AM and I Claim it Now.

Thus will you see and know the awesome weave of the true benevolence of Creation, and you will bask in this benevolence, in this inner knowing, in seeing this manifest within and all around you. And in this way, you will lift up everything and everyone you touch, everyone you think of. You will Know that you have Birthed the Divine Child of the Universe within your core.

~ 25 December, 2007

Victim consciousness is the inner programming that says, "I can't, poor me, I am helpless, I am controlled, I must control and manipulate. I will never....I am helpless and hopeless....woe is me....everything is too hard..."

Victory consciousness says, I Can! I AM! I Know! I Will!

Poverty consciousness is the programming that says, "I don't have enough, there is not enough, I am not enough, I am not good enough, I must save and slave and scrimp, I must hold tightly to what I have, I am worthless, I do not deserve, I am shame, I have not "measured up", I am less than...... "

Abundance consciousness says, "All that my Mother-Father God has is mine, All is Well, all is beauty, there is enough and more than enough of everything for everyone. Mother Earth, in all her natural beauty, my creative spirit, and my community provides all I will ever need."

Conditional love only loves the reflection of what it has been programmed to love or hate. It is based on having one's needs fulfilled and only on it's own terms. It is limited, possessive, full of illusion, fear, and trying to change others because one does not themselves feel loved or lovable just as they are.

Unconditional love loves All That Is - every person, rock, tree, and animal as one love. Unconditional love is humble and non-judgmental, always learning more about others and oneself. It is a Way of Being, sharing, connecting, expanding, and feeling fulfilled.

Lust consciousness means insatiable greed, spiritual emptiness and longing. It says: I need, I can never get enough to fill this hole, I am empty, I am nothing, I need and want *more* of everything/anything, and I must "have".

Unity consciousness feels and knows that ALL is One, equal *and* unique. Unity consciousness celebrates ones' self and the glorious diversity of creation expressing.

Chapter 6

Who – or What is The Magdalene?

"I am the first. I am the last. I am the one who has been scorned. And I am the one who has been honored. I am the whore and the one who is holy. I am the wife and I am the virgin. I am the mother, and I am the daughter. I am the one who has not conceived, yet many are my sons." ~ from *The Thunder, Perfect Mind*, The Nag Hammadi Scrolls

"I AM here, there, and everywhere. I AM Here at the end and at the beginning, at the beginning and the end. Always present. Omnipresent. And so are You." ~ The Magdalene

The Magdalene represents the Feminine Christ. Historically she shared Yeshua's lineage within the mystical Jewish communities of The Essenes, who revered Father God and the Divine Mother - the divine feminine in all life. Many Essenes, including both Yeshua and Magdalene were also initiates of the Egyptian Isis-Osiris Mystery Schools, and studied with spiritual masters even into India and the British Isles. Magdalene was also historically the teacher of the teachers, as she knew, through Gnosis or direct knowing, all that Yeshua knew and taught. They were one mind, one heart, one soul, and one being. And simultaneously, they were human and man and woman. She and Yeshua came to the Earth Plane together, along with many others, to plant seeds of love, light, truth, wisdom, healing and freedom.

The Essenes lived in community; ate mostly raw foods from their gardens and orchards; worked with the angels of the air, water, fire, earth, stars; honored women and children; and celebrated life and honored Creator and the Divine Mother through song and dance and ceremony. Women and men were equals, and men's first responsibility was to protect and care for the beloved women and children of the communities.

Yeshua and Mary came here as a team, as a demonstration of unity consciousness, and as enlightened beings who were to seed this planet with the seeds of love, light, wisdom and freedom that would blossom forth 2,000+ years later, in the next great precession of the equinoxes - The Aquarian Age. Humanity was going to go through much suffering in those 2,000 years. Suffering caused by fear and ignorance, by manipulation and deception, by wars and violence - by separation. This separation was felt as separation from God or Source; separation within the self through confusion, turmoil and inner conflict - being "divided"; separation from and judgment of others - especially those who were different in any way; and separation between nations and cultures.

This suffering would ultimately allow each human being to embark on a personal journey of self-realization, which would cause each one to choose anew - to choose Life, to choose Love, and to choose Peace. While the two fish symbolized the Piscean Age, the Aquarian Age is symbolized by the Water Bearer, each person pouring forth their waters of love and illumination for benefit of all others. The esoteric keynotes for the Age of Pisces was "I Believe". The keynote for the Aquarian Age is "I Know".

The Magdalene and The Christ came together into the lifetime in Palestine, along with many Masters of love, the Essenes, to anchor energies within the 'physics' of the earth - from the physical dirt, to all life here, to all the energy fields of all consciousness on the planet which were to blossom forth in the coming Age of Aquarius. The seeds of love that were planted in full consciousness then have matured through this 2,000+ year cycle, and humanity has learned so much about love - the entire spectrum from self-hatred and hatred of others to love in all of it many splendid forms. The dispensation for this new age, this next 2,000 year cycle, is Freedom. This age will be for exploring all the reasons why humanity was given the gift of free will, which is a Universal Law, and to explore the many facets of Freedom, as we have explored many facets of Love.

Magdalene is also the 4th aspect of YWYH - Yod He (Hey) Vod He (Hey) - which represents God the Father, The Divine Mother - Sophia, The Christ (son) and The Magdalene (daughter). The Magdalene is part of the Office of The Christ and is one of the Ascended Masters of our planet who is responsible for activating The Christ who lives in every human heart. She, along with many others, is an activator of Divine Love, Wisdom and Truth, strength and gentleness, and passion for the awakening of inner truth and cosmic sovereignty in every soul that has emanated from the heart of God.

Both Yeshua and Mary were also very human, experiencing the whole spectrum of what it is to be human. What they were demonstrating was what we are all experiencing now: the complete human-divine merge and the glory of that grand design! The Gnostic stories say that when The Christ ascended, The Magdalene vowed to be born in to every generation as a woman from that time until this day now. She has, like every Mother, experienced the entire spectrum of what it is to be human - every nook and cranny, from every angle. This is why the Gnostics have been waiting for the time they call The Reception of the Bride; which is when the fullness, the full spectrum of who Mary Magdalene was, and who she is and always will be is finally seen in the light of day without persecution or misunderstanding.

There is a stained glass at Kilmore Church on the Isle of Mull in Scotland that has become very well known in the past few years. It shows Yeshua and pregnant Magdalene. This symbolism can be found in many chapels and cathedrals, especially in France and the British Isles where many of these chapels were built by The Knights Templar, who were protectors of The Magdalene teachings, the true teachings of The Christ - The Book of Love. Mary Magdalene and other Essene teachers spread the wisdom practices of The Book of Love widely throughout France, the British Isles, and Eastern Europe.

These teachings were deemed heretical and followers of these teachings had to "go underground". This includes The Essenes, The Cathars, The Knights Templar, the

Druids, and the Gnostics. This is why this knowledge became "the hidden mysteries" both during and after Yeshua's lifetime. Various inquisitions of The Roman Church destroyed every remnant of these groups that could be found. This was reiterated and repeated with indigenous peoples around the world who honor Earth Mother and the feminine aspects of Creator and Creation.

Chapter 7

The Book of Love
Activities of the Christos-Sophia

We Come to remind you, to reflect to you That Which You Are. We see each of you as That Which We Are: Divine Eternal Love, Peace, and Truth. We are not only your mirror, but Who You Are.

We came at the inception of the Piscean Age, after thousands of years of preparation by and assistance from thousands of Beings of Light, to seed every particle and sub-atomic particle of Gaia with the Love and Truth that We Are.

At the time of the crucifixion, we traveled in spirit to all levels, all dimensions of all hells and all heavens – to "the many mansions" of states of consciousness to seed Light, to seed Love, to seed Truth, and to seed Unity.

At the time of the Resurrection, All Life, every particle of Life was Liberated to blossom forth at the inception of the next age – the Age of Aquarius. Now is the Time of Blossoming – the Age of Flowers – the Age of Creativity – the Age of Known and Felt ONE-ness of All That Is.

At the inception of the Piscean Age, the Divine Masculine Aspect of the ONE that We Are, was the outward manifestation of All That Is: " I and My Father are ONE." At that time, women were subservient in many cultures, and so the Divine Feminine aspect of All That Is, All of Creation which come from the Void, the Womb, where All Creation is Birthed; was suppressed. The power of feminine love in all its forms was denied by the religions of the time and those that would be constructed.

The Truth is that the Christed Yeshua and the Magdalene were and are ONE Being, and WE have always been this. This is why in the Gnostic Gospels, the Nag Hammadi scrolls, and all the revelations of Truth that are continuing to emerge through many voices were not "uncovered" or spoken, except in secret, until this past century, preceding the Dawn of Aquarius. The teachings in these revealed gospels, fragments, teachings and oral traditions tell of Yeshua continually pointing to the Magdalene as the Sophia – the Great Mother – Creation Herself who encompasses ALL of Creation in Love – All has been Birthed from Her and All Returns to be Birthed from Her again.

We Come Now, at the inception of the Aquarian Age, in the outward manifestation of the Divine Feminine Aspect, the Great Mother who loves each and every ONE with a great love, a love that is all-encompassing and all-embracing – that honors each of you and all of your seeming mistakes and errors and mis-creations because the Truth is that everything has had a purpose.

The purpose of each human Being experiencing the spectrum of darkness to light was for a Great Purpose, as it results in true compassion and all-encompassing understanding and love. It results in unshakeable spiritual strength and sovereignty.

We ask you to allow yourself to Be who you truly are: all-encompassing and all-embracing Love. Claim your Planetary, Galactic, Universal, and Cosmic Sovereignty; and through this claiming, transform your reality in an Instant! And let the fun begin!

This Love is exciting. It is nourishing. It is Eternal. It is creative. It knows no "wrong". It makes no one else wrong. Its signature is unity, harmony, and integrity. It is alignment. It is wholeness.

~ 25 December, 2007

Chapter 8

Activities of The Christos-Sophia Part Two

We are the Christ Consciousness, which is blossoming forth on earth now. There are multitudes of Christed humans who live in Christ Consciousness, and who are joining with the Christed beings from all corners of creation: a great extended family of light who have come to join and assist with anchoring and implementing the new Planetary, Galactic, Universal and Cosmic Dispensation of Ascension, Love, Peace, Freedom, Truth, and Creativity. The true nature of who we are and who you are- the Divine Human, is being birthed in each individuated soul here now. Please look in the mirror at the stars in your eyes, at the love in your eyes, and see the Christos-Sophia there.

Why has The Christos-Sophia come now to speak with strength and passion in a female form? It is time for truth, for equality, for balance, for gentleness, for passion, for the nurturing of the divine creative spirit within each being of life on this planet. It is the time for utter truth to not only be told, but To Be. It is the completion of the mission begun in Palestine more than 2,000 years ago, and of many eons of cycles of time in which the Divine Plan would work out to it's completion through all the kingdoms and queendoms of creation - and that time is now.

The Christos-Sophia comes in the female form to remind each soul, who has suffered in the suppression of the beautiful feminine qualities of unconditional love, beauty, sensuality, nurturing, and nourishment that The Christ is Feminine as well as masculine. She comes to liberate the love of and respect for the feminine energy and of the children. She comes to honor all the life forms of Beloved Gaia. In truth, she has never left. She is all manifested creation.

Chapter 9

The Goodness Vision for A Brighter World

I AM here, there, and everywhere.
I AM Here at the end and at the beginning,
at the beginning and the end.
Always present. Omnipresent. And so are you.

~ The Magdalene

Awaken Great Spirits and Flesh – Humankind!

Now is the time to Live.

Now is the time to smell and taste the fruits of Gaia – to swell in her pregnant rapture, to sit with her in circles of nourishment, to reclaim your true nature – as suns and daughters of Love, of Light, of Power, of Compassion, of Joy and Ecstasy dancing with the wind, and clouds, with the light on all waters throughout Gaia – the dance of life and love – the Rapture.

Raise yourselves from the slumbers of forgetting – this forgetting is all of the pain you have taken on of all here that has been less than perfect, less than perfect love. Flail yourselves no longer. Give Mother Love to your heart, to your mother, to the mother within. Give mother love to the lost little boy within you, to the baby crying in her crib, to the confusion of plastic toys and plastic diapers and plastic smiles, and words that do not match the vibrations of truth deep within your heart flame. Fan the flames of your heart, of your vision, of your Paradise Here again Now.

I AM calling for you to share the joy of your hearts with me,

to share your vision and hope for the future with me.

Bring your Joy back to the heart of the Mother and she will amplify it and send it back, circulating and circulating it in to the fabric of your cells and atoms as they resonate in great harmonies of Love washing through all of creation in the same moment, through all layers of dimensions, through every frequency which now resounds with the simplicity of Love.

Empty your pain, empty it out until you feel yourself a hollow bone ready to receive all resonating frequencies all at once, till your dreams come true, till you see the Great Beloved in every atom of existence.

Humanity!

You are intended to live your Greatness–
the Greatness of the human Spirit within you aligned with the Greatness of Divinity Within.

This spirit is Creativity Itself, ever forming itself anew – ever bringing forth more love, more beauty, more inspiration and upliftment for all forms of life – here and throughout all the Universes.

The current turning point is all around us; on every hand we see the futility, pain, and despair of illusion – the surreal effects of deception which manufacture war, environmental destruction, and the severe limiting of the spirit of our children.

In our hearts, none of us wants this kind of society, this kind of living – and yet we have been programmed to believe that we must follow the rules even though we all remember that we never understood them! We do not need health insurance, car insurance, and life insurance – which are all based on making money on people's fears of survival and of catastrophe, and of death. We do not need debt which capitalizes daily, keeping us distracted with all the illusions that have been created, marketed, and made into law.

We can heal everything with Love, Light and intention or prayer – the power inherent in each of us, that which we are made of, the likeness of the creator of All That Is, which is also What We Are!

~ May, 2007

Shaman's Cave, Sedona AZ

Chapter 10

The Inner Child

Beloved Sisters and Brothers of the One Great Heart! It is such a great pleasure to be with you Here Now, together. You have come, at this time of Cosmic Transition, Transformation and Transfiguration with great promise, skills, and gifts!

Today, we want to bring forth from the subconscious, and heal, your inner child. We want to retrieve so many parts of you that early on in your life became buried in avalanches of neglect. You see, all of you were born from the Glory of the higher realms of light, of vast consciousness, innate and unspeakable understanding, and vast deep wells of wisdom and love. And no one here on the earth plane saw you for that which you were, and are. No one greeted you as an honored and eternal being of love, light, power, wisdom, creativity and joy. This is, of course, because these understandings had been lost through countless generations.

Some of you were seen and felt as a curse, some as a burden, some were abused, some neglected because the veils of ignorance go back far into the annals of time. Often the adults whose world you entered were caught up in themselves and their problems, worries, and work. Many of you were loved and nurtured, but not truly seen or understood for the full consciousness and intelligence that you are and were from the womb onward. You were "just babies" who could not yet speak, and so the great intelligence, sensitivity, compassion, and love that you came to give were rejected. Essentially, this is how it felt to you as a newcomer to this world – because you were not truly seen, you felt rejected, and on top of that you felt it must be your fault. You see, as I have said many times before – you are Love in a Human Form, and because at birth and in the earliest years you are pure love and sensitivity, the love that you are feels something is wrong and takes on responsibility for that disconnection. Some in your environment would perhaps momentarily catch a glimpse of eternity, of wisdom, of the vast unconditional love available through you, through your eyes, through your energy fields – and yet, it would be usually forgotten and slip into unconsciousness once more. This glimpse of eternity could only happen if the mother or father or relative was *fully* present in the moment. So, you have all, for the most part, experienced not being seen, heard or felt; which translates in your emotional world as not being valued, thus not having value, and certainly not having value for simply Being You. Your childhood and teen and often adult years then become a long distance race to either prove that you are valuable or to rebel and self-destruct.

Now, please take a deep Breath, and another – and another. Allow yourself to feel the tragedy of this predicament for yourselves and all your sisters and brothers. Feel the loss. Feel the emptiness that you have desperately or methodically tried to fill with everything under the sun. Feel the enormous love, the thunder and lightening of your vast intelligence, all that you have had to offer your world – all the possibilities that have gone to waste. Feel the grief of this.

Now, please Breathe in Love – the Love the cosmos has for *you* in all your eternal Glory – and Breathe out Peace. Again, Breathe in cosmic Love – Breathe out Peace. And again – Breathe in Love, Breath out Peace. Continue to breathe in this way until you feel the love and peace deeply relaxing your mind, body and soul.

Now, I invite you to envision and to feel your world as a place of honoring each divine child, each divine human. View the vistas of invitation, of possibilities explored and realized, of perfection. See and feel the great symphony of creativity coming forth from people who know they are loved, seen, honored and valued.

Please take your consciousness back to the moments before your birth and allow no drugs, no forceps, no cold surfaces, or harsh lights, or unconscious hands or hearts to meet you. See yourself birthing into the arms of loving, aware, awake Mothers and Fathers – see their love and wonder and amazement and joy that you have come in to their lives. Feel how they feel you as a miracle. Feel secure that they will honor you as you grow and explore and become more and more fully self-realized, self-actualized.

Reclaim your precious self! See and feel yourself as a young child – confident, joyful, playful, and ready for anything! See and feel yourself following your own inner guidance, exploring all that delights you, feeling your amazing physical body full of exuberant life force energy that no one tries to stifle! You are not sitting inside four walls in hard seats or glued to the television set or computer screen. You are running and playing, learning about Mother Earth, singing, being with animals and friends, learning about all the things you love on this beautiful Mother, Earth. See yourself as you discover more and more and more about yourself and the world around you. See yourself as a teenager and feel yourself exploring and expanding your unique creative gifts - reaching further inward and expanding the parameters of yourself. Feel the glory of all you know, all you are learning and experiencing, the stunning beauty of yourself. Feel your creative gifts flowing through you with joy and passion and being received with joy by your family, friends, and communities.

We are here to *create* this reality. We are here today to deeply understand that each baby entering this planet is a great soul who has journeyed forever in many worlds, including this one, time after time after time after time. Acknowledge yourself and all of your sisters and brothers, all of the children on beloved Mother Earth for journeying through galaxies, and universes, and planets and coming to this planet now as a culminating gift to this planet and to each of us as we create and anchor the New Earth together.

Each baby and young child that we recognize, nurture, and allow to unfold in all his or her glory is a gift to all of us now and far into the future. We do this Now for our own inner child. As you are *fully present* by choice, you choose this great gift of the fullness of life as a way of life, as a gift to life. Each of you is God-Goddess in action, evolving everything. Each of you is in the process of "marrying" the Human and the Divine within the human vehicle with its vast abilities to sense and feel and think and act – to relish all the pleasures of Life on Mother Earth.

Each of you can choose this activity of Creation to be a dance of love, of fulfillment, of the juiciness and richness of the creative spirit flowing and flowering in fields of delights – the New Earth emerging through each of you.

And so, allow these visions to entice you to have reverence and awe and tenderness and joy for your inner child – the infant, the toddler, and the young child you were and still are in your essence. Allow your discomfort, disillusionment, desolation, devastation and anger just dissolve away in to the past, as you choose to create your self, your world, and your experiences Now, every moment. As you claim you back for you now, you claim life for every precious being on our precious Earth, and She laughs and dances and sings along with you forevermore.

~February 25, 2011

My brother David in Boynton Canyon
Sedona AZ

Chapter 11

2012, Ascension & the 7th Golden Age

May we each be deeply nourished by Cosmic Love, in, through, and as us. May we infuse our whole human family, all our relations, and Gaia, with love as our hearts overflow with gratitude.

Good Evening! We are grateful to be here together in this ancient sacred site where so many great ones have walked and walk again today. Tonight, we share simple truths for this most auspicious time throughout creation. We represent the feminine Christ aspects of Christ Consciousness. Like us, each of you is an eternal androgynous being who carries the divine trinity within. You are divine masculine and feminine alchemically birthing the divine child, your authentic self. You carry the codes of truth within your heart. You *are* truth, just as you *are* love in a human body. You are love, loving All That Is. You are truth being revealed.

2012 is a cosmic trigger encoded into every human heart, timed to this most awe-inspiring shift of the ages. Ascension spirals, advancing to the next octave, forever expanding. The most important message at this time is to release the past Beloved ones – release everything. Allow your selves to empty and go into the Void, to the stillness. Be simply fully present here now. Now is the time to claim the fullness of your divinity and the fullness of your humanity merging completely here now. This is the fulfillment and culmination of a divine plan.

At this time cycles within cycles are coming to completion and grand cycles are opening and birthing. Each individuated soul has journeyed for a very long time in many universes and worlds including Beloved Gaia. Your heritage *is* this grand design, and yet the most important thing at this time is who you are *now*. Who you are now embodies all you have ever been.

And so we are asking you now, if you will, to release all attachments. The more that you can release all physical and emotional trauma, painful memories, resentments, and the glamour of past identities; the more you will be fully present as your great I AM now.

Humanity has been programmed for guilt, shame, fear, abandonment, betrayal, and victim consciousness. It is time to delete this conditioning from the past and let your self be free. This particular lifetime has been long and arduous, full of many deaths and rebirths, as psychodynamics that needed to be resolved by each of you were completed as your gift to Creator. You were charged with the great task of resolving all that was out of balance, out of synch, out of love. So, the willingness to face and embrace the darkness within yourself as part of your wholeness is very important to the culmination of the divine plan when each of you could *freely choose* to be a cosmic, sovereign being. You could not be fully realized God-Goddess Beings walking this planet until you chose to be free, until with freedom you *chose* love and the full expression of divinity after many cycles of experiencing darkness and light within and around you.

Learning to let go with an open hand, learning to deeply love while being detached, is the current theme for humanity right now. You cannot move fully into the 7th Golden Age until you are truly willing to let go of the past: the past month, the past moment, the past breath. As the timelines continue to collapse toward the omega point, an intricate layering of synchronicities, timelines, past and parallel lives are coming together as you enter ever more fully into unity consciousness. There are almost 8 billion beautiful souls on Gaia, each with a unique and personal spiritual path. You are coming together in the simple truth of the one heart. You are eternal beings, cosmic citizens forever creating, re-creating, and co-creating. Allow the dream to be dreamed, unfolded, and realized through you – moment to moment.

The Piscean Age comes to an end. Your sacred world is full of holy babies and holy children who are raising the frequencies of your beautiful planet with their love and light. As your solar system dances through space and aligns with the Great Central Spiritual Sun, the magnetic heart center of your galaxy, you all are embraced by the in-breath of God. All of creation is vibrating faster and higher, becoming ever more enlightened and harmonious as the 7th Golden Age emerges every moment. *Welcome* to the 7th Golden Age of Peace and Love and Creativity!

~ July 21, 2011

Glastonbury, England

Painting of Gaia's Alignment with

The Great Central Sun

artist unknown

Chapter 12

This Precious Time of Day

This precious time of day!

As the birds sing goodnight

to the golden sun, she

brings forth her brilliance-

flaming red deepening to violet -

evening palette shining on the

sweet red rocks here in this City of Light.

The richness of these moments!

Delicious love play of sun, moon, and earth -

their language of joy spreads out in

spectrums of colors and songs

sweeping towards a night filled with stars.

And then, more bliss,

and fullness of heart as

the western clouds in the violet sky

begin their evening glow of impossible shining pink!

~ August 9, 2011

Sedona, AZ

Chapter 13

We Reclaim this Precious Planet Now

We reclaim this precious jewel of a planet *Now*, to be a Universal Home, sharing great beauty and joy and emotion-filled artistic celebration and community with all Galactic and Universal guests who seek to bask in Gaia's beauty among the richness of an enlightened humanity.

The Red Spring at Chalice Well Gardens

Glastonbury, England

Chapter 14

Greetings from the Heart of Creator

Greetings from the Heart of Creator and your excited Council of Love. You are recalibrating your bodies to accept the fullness of your Cosmic Christ-Magdalene Presence in all glory so that you may shine as a galactic sun and bring humanity upward and upward in to the realms of Truth with each breath each one takes.

Yes, you are a telepathic communicator and all that you know is flowing on waves through humanity's consciousness - to allow the fertile ground of new ways of living and being to come forth for the glory of Gaia, this galaxy, the Federations of Light, and all ascended beings through all time-spaces. Rest and recalibrate. Sleep and nap. Drink water. Breathe sunlight and freshen the atmosphere with each breath of Love's essence carrying the telepathic messages that are received in the loosening spaces within humanity's opening minds and hearts. This is making possible each one's attunement to the guidance of their soul, which is registered and entertained, as each one's perception moves in to new vistas of possibility and creativity.

Sing unto this day while you are embodied here.

Spread molecules of freedom.

Flow these through the atmosphere of the entire planet.

Stand in brilliance.

Breath love, in and out.

Receive!

Pomegranate Heart on Red Rock, Sedona

Chapter 15

The Christ-Magdalene Song of Spring

Our voices ripple to you over the waves of time/space, through dimensions of untold beauties. Our voices speak with you now and you will feel wondrous bells tinkling within, as these beauties and truths are encoded within your heart since you were birthed forth from the Heart of Creator. Your consciousness is eternal, and plays in many spaces, places, times, and dimensions throughout the many layers and vistas of creation - forever.

Soul Card by Jewels

from an original artwork by Pamela Becker

Chapter 16

All Is Well

Greetings from the Heart and Soul of Who You Are. We Are The Christ-Magdalene, also known as The Christos-Sophia. We hold the cosmic patterns of the Christ Consciousness of Love, Wisdom and Truth, which reside in your heart and in every cell of your beautiful divine being.

We begin with the prayer reverberating from the Heart of Creator and Creation - "All Is Well". All is *very* well. The rising consciousness and the ever-expanding Love from the heart and soul of humankind is creating ripples of great joy in the eternal oceans of Cosmic Consciousness as you each free yourselves to enjoy the knowing, feeling, and experiences of unity and harmony. As each of you enter into these states of consciousness individually and as families and groups, the joy reverberates through creation and all that lives everywhere, affecting every-ONE with ecstatic celebration.

We choose to speak with you through the written word at this time as all is ripe now for the deep embrace of the Divine Feminine aspect of the Christ Consciousness and for the Great Mother, birther and sustainer of All That Is Everywhere, to be felt and known. The divine fire, the breath of Life, Light, Intelligence, and "The Force" of creativity is birthed through the Great Mother who is ever-evolving manifestation - the forms and interplay of All That Is. As what has been hidden behind "the veil" now comes forth through the great divine Gaia and all her life forms, humankind finds and feels the overwhelming Love of the Divine Mother and an exquisite serenity, security and safety continues to displace all feelings and experiences of separation, abandonment, and fear. All ONE of Us, throughout creation, awakes with joy and peace to each new morning and the New Day is Born in love and connection - At-One-Ment, with All That Is.

Yes, I, who is called The Magdalene-Sophia, AM Here with you. I AM the very fabric of your being, woven into every particle, energy meridian, every feeling and every heartbeat. I AM Love, and *you are love.* There is no separation. Any and all separation you have ever felt, experienced and believed in is merely mental and emotional programming. It is what you have been taught and what you have learned in this grand experiment in forgetting all of who you are. You have journeyed through many lives of ignorance and fear, divorced from the truth of who you truly are in essence and expression.

Now is the time to freely and spontaneously express the joy and the deep love that weaves throughout the fabric of your being and to celebrate yourself, your life, and each other.

~ April 2012, Sedona AZ

Our New Sun

Chimney Rock~The Tor, Sedona

Christmas Day 2010

Chapter 17

The Feminine Christing of Humanity

On Magdalene's Feast Day, July 22 of 2009, Mary Magdalene channeled that this day represented the Feminine Christing of Humanity. Yeshua was over lighted by and integrated with The Cosmic Christ at the Baptism initiation, and then demonstrated the Piscean keynotes for the next three years through the Transfiguration, Resurrection and Ascension. July 2009 was the beginning of the three years of demonstrating and anchoring the keynotes of the next cycle – The Age of Aquarius, The Age of Flowers, and setting the energies of The New Earth, when all of humanity will Self-Realize that they are The Christ Consciousness, The Unified Heart– One Family loving and supporting each other and our Mother Earth.

This is the time when The Rainbow Nation emerges - one beautiful humanity in more than 7 billion beautiful individualities - joined together telepathically through the Unified Heart and Soul. We have already begun! We are already in the beginning stages of the 7th Golden Age on beautiful Gaia! The Age of Flowers comes forth rapidly in resplendent beauty, wisdom, love and truth!

Rejoice and Be Glad!

Stained glass window in Salisbury Cathedral, England
Two of "The Marys"

Mary of Bethany and Mary Magdalene

Chapter 18

The Goddess

The Divine Feminine has infinite names and faces throughout the eons on beloved Mother Earth and throughout time and the cosmos. If you ask me who I AM, I will tell you, "I AM ALL That Is". And so are you. I AM One with myself, with you, with the One Human Family. I AM One with the trees and the birds, the oceans, rivers, streams and rocks. I AM One with the Masters and all our star sisters and brothers; all the angels, fairies, and elves: all the kingdoms and queendoms of Mother Earth and of all worlds and systems everywhere throughout this vast and glorious creation! I AM One with every aspect of creation in all its glorious and diverse beauty.

Are you One with me? Are you One with yourself and all your beloved friends and family, pets and flowers, birds and butterflies? As you give yourself the great gift of letting go of all the parts of you that have been hiding; your shame and guilt and pain and judgments; when you love and forgive yourself and all others and all situations of injustice and despair - you enter the eternal flow of divine love and the illumination of divine light and your divine wild child - your spontaneous creativity is free to be, to express, and to love All That Is. This is what your child, and all the children are showing us Now. Your child will show you this purely and in utter delight if you are At-One with yourself and if you honor yourself by loving yourself.

When you *know* you are love, loving All That Is, you enter the eternal flow of unconditional love, Christ Consciousness and the embrace of Mother-Father God and Peace Reigns in every heart and throughout our precious Mother Earth, the solar system of which she is the heart, the Milky Way Galaxy and all our neighbors, and beyond through eternity and infinity.

Mother and Child, Chalice Well Gardens

Glastonbury, England

Chapter 19

The Rise of the Divine Feminine and the Fall of the Global Economy

The rise of the Divine Feminine is pulsing from the Heart of the Great Central Spiritual Sun, which is the magnetic heart of our Milky Way Galaxy - a place that nourishes all star systems here with great love. The divine feminine is fully on the planet now. The Earth herself is an embodiment of the feminine, and the desecration of Mother Earth is a mirror of the disregard for the feminine that has been so prevalent here for many cycles of time and experience. However, the divine feminine is capable of loving anyone and everyone no matter what. She has seen, been, done it all. She IS all, all of creation embodied in every particle of energy that makes Life, and because she is intimate with All, the divine feminine spirit can embrace everything and everyone with compassion and understanding and respect for each soul's free will choices, as each soul lives and learns on the path of becoming One - At-One with one's self, At-One with each other, At-One with All That Is. This is the knowledge and the wisdom of the heart. This is the peace of letting go and surrendering to the flow of love and life. This is the humility and the bliss of recognizing the divine in everyone and everything.

The 11:11:11 (Nov. 11, 2011) gateway expanded the energies from the Great Central Sun coming to Gaia, humanity, and all life here. Each person who feels and expands these energies brings forth the beautiful divine qualities of the masculine as well, as these higher and lighter vibrations are androgynous - One. In the mystery schools of Isis, of which the Magdalene and many other Essene women and men were initiates and adepts, the way of love was that the woman is the initiatress who shows men how to love -whether it is mother love, friendship love, community love, sexual love. In the goddess mystery schools throughout the world, the priestesses were the initiators of teaching men how to love woman and children, of bringing forth the best from each being so communities would flourish and thrive in happiness and well-being for all.

When women deeply and truly trust their Beloved, when they feel truly honored, cherished, and adored; the benefits and goodness and beauty of the woman comes forth in fullness. When women are truly loved, children are happy, secure, can grow through their unique creative gifts, and know how to love and be loved.

Redistribution of the Wealth of Mother Earth

The redistribution of the wealth of the planet to all nations and each person equally and utter debt forgiveness for individuals and countries is a pre-requisite for the full ascension for all of humanity, and will be coming forth in this auspicious year of transformation. It is an absolutely necessary reconfiguration of what has been out of balance in the very core of civilizations on earth for many cycles of time. As the wonderful teacher, Patricia Cota-Robles (www.eraofpeace.org) has said for many years, we really cannot have peace on the planet without simultaneously having prosperity. This is because the disparity and suffering having to do with lack, insecurity, enslavement, and distractions having to do with money goes so deep and is so multi-faceted. Money has created so much separation in every conceivable way. It has created a state of inequality, fear, lack, and enslavement that is so insidious and so woven in to our cultures, our "reality" and our life streams- that until humanity is liberated from that whole scenario, peace cannot truly come to the planet.

There is a multitude of ways that money has affected humanity's beliefs and feelings about themselves and others - everything from survival fears to caste systems of all kinds, to feelings of inferiority or superiority, to the buying and selling of women, children, the natural resources of Mother Earth, to the creation of so many things that are unnecessary and even damaging to life, health and happiness.

The complete redistribution of the wealth of this planet to every woman, man and child has to come forth because the clarion call of Creator and of Sophia is that this is the time for humanity and the planet to ascend into the 5th dimensional New Earth and that really cannot happen without both prosperity and peace. All of humanity needs to feel the joy and freedom that financial security will bring to each and every one. The energies of joy and peace which will arise from every person having all they need are part of the energies of ascension and will boost the ascension process for humanity as a whole, as well as giving great relief to Mother Earth herself.

Prosperity and peace and freedom are a free will choice, and each person needs to make this choice for himself or herself. Then the tsunami of relief for humanity as a whole to become truly equal will roll through the planet on waves of joy and liberation. You see, the spreading of the wealth equally creates true equality from the very source of what has been gross inequality and a gross mechanism of control and fear. All the things that will "come falling down", that will dissolve in to the past - the misperceptions, mis-creations, mis-aligments, distortions and deceptions will come down and are coming down right now.

Everywhere across the whole planet the young people are rising up now and saying no more - we know what is happening - we know what is untrue here and out of integrity and is unfair and unjust and unnecessary -and we do not choose this anymore. We choose community, creativity, love, sharing - we choose Life, which is to live fully and freely - for one and for all.

The television and entertainment industry has caused people to live vicariously, living a fantasy of other people's lives in little pieces of light coming off a screen. These technologies have been a way of programming people to not live. These technologies have been a tool of mental and emotional programming; using techniques of subliminal programming of the subconscious to create states of fear, insecurity, false desire, greed, and distortion of the truth. Mother Earth in all her beauty, connection with the divine spirit in all things, and human creativity are the true forms of joy, fulfillment, and belonging.

Anchor deeply within you the unshakeable knowing that you are love and that love is all there is. Embody this love fully, connected with Mother Earth ~ Gaia, on every level - physical, etheric (your energy body or aura), emotional and mental (these are also energy bodies). Because everything is energy, all of our bodies are energetic and interpenetrating with the physical and etheric bodies. All the different layers of our energy bodies are imprinted with information, tendencies, past experiences, and more.

Embody and be love. Another anchor is to completely trust yourself - trusting all of who you are, trusting all that comes through you, trusting every particle of you - what you say, feel, think, dream. When you trust yourself, you are gentle and kind to yourself and then to others. Another anchor is creativity - letting "the force" flow - being who you really are - being your authentic self - letting your Christed Self be all you are in every moment. And this is how you can both demonstrate and model freedom and authenticity as a way of living in joy; and be a shining example of what being a divine human looks and feels like.

Any time we can feel the love flowing through us, we send it to the planetary grids and humanity's consciousness as a whole, as one being of consciousness, as one heart beating as one with Mother Earth. All of the highest thoughts that we have, the greatest love that comes through us, the greatest revelations we have inside of us get translated into the collective consciousness of humanity and raises humanity's consciousness literally in frequency, illumination, enlightenment, and love. It is a service to creation to simply be you.

Quiet yourself; go into stillness, breath in golden-white opalescent light for several minutes. Then open your eyes - and when you open them, the world will seem brighter and you will feel more expanded and lighter. This brightness and feeling of deep peace and expansiveness is always there. We are weaving dimensions, strengthening The Rainbow Bridge.

So every time we see 5th dimensional light and color, we are permeating the dimensions and opening up the rainbow bridge just that much more until all can see and live in the 5th dimensional frequencies of love, unity, harmony, creativity, peace and joy.

Part of the divine feminine is the darkness, the void, the great mystery, the black hole, the womb of creation from which everything is born and to which everything returns to be reconfigured into new forms. Fear of going in to the void, in to dynamic change, into the mystery, in to the New Earth is simply programming that you can rise above. Shifting focus and being brave and visionary, we dream the New Earth into form through our deepest truth within. The joy and peace and fulfillment you desire for your children and your children's children will be revealed and will be the new way of life.

As your heart continues to expand and soften, you know that there is no such thing as ever being alone. You know and feel your connection with every particle of life through all forms. You are one with the Divine

Mother and Father, the dark and the light, the night and the day, the sun and the stars, with All That Is. There is no judgment left in you, no separation from yourself or others or Mother-Father God or any part of creation. You have risen! You have risen above duality, judgment, persecution, loneliness, fear, and lack into a higher and brighter way of being reflected back to you in a higher and brighter life.

Coming Transformation in Politics

The coming change in politics, most simply, is that anything that is not continuing to expand to a higher vibration is going to dissolve. So anywhere there are governments that are based in greed, violence, betrayal and deception as opposed to the good of the people as a whole and the planet herself will be dissolving away as each person and humanity as a whole choose to live in love and peace and the truth of who we are. We are Planetary Citizens of a precious jewel, and her stewards. We are One Family with incredible diversity to enjoy and share. The plants and animals, the oceans and mountains - every thing on Earth is precious and we can and will enjoy it all together.

The new generation - the idealistic, intelligent, creative indigo children are ready to step into their empowerment, their creative ideas and their ways to create the New Earth. They are ready all over the world to step in to this. We can support them with our consciousness, prayers, and physical support. We can support their efforts, their ideas, their love, their spirit and their creativity. These young people need to be heard and seen and supported to do what their passions are, what they came to do. If all people on Gaia had been supported in being who they truly are for generations, we would be living in a peaceful world now. And this is the world humanity is now choosing to create. This is the fruit of the divine plan for humanity. This is being cheered on by all of our family of light everywhere, and Creator smiles in fulfillment.

~ December 2, 2011

Group channeling in Sedona

Quan Yin face from full scale sculpture -

Andrea Smith Gallery, Sedona AZ

Chapter 20

Beloved Eternal Family of Gaia

We bid you a warm hello on this pristine summer day when the clouds are puffy and sweet in a clear, clear blue sky, warm breezes lift the leaves of the trees as they dance in the sunlight, chickadees sing to their friends and quail coo to their families, and lizards leap from branch to rock. You are blessed to live on beautiful Gaia, and we ask you to relish her beauty, to make sure that you yourselves and all the children of the planet enjoy great intimacy with Mother Earth and all her life forms. There is no technology that can match the colors of the flowers, the rainbows, the changing colors of the moon each night, or any living thing - as the colors of all Living things are made with love and light, in perfection, through divine intelligence.

Gaia's beauty is soothing, healing, familiar, and ecstatic. She brings peace to the mind, joy to the heart, and pleasure to all the senses. The more you know her beauty; the more this is all you will see. As the joy of this focus, and your ever increasing awe in feeling oneness with her magnificence expands and expands, those man-made blights on her landscapes will fade and dissolve as the New Earth is seen more richly by more and more beloveds souls - so that poetry and song spring from your hearts! Send your love to the bees, the polar bears, the tigers and every creature that lives here with you, that they may feel your welcome, so they will feel seen and known and loved deeply for who they are and how they contribute to the majesty of Mother Earth.

Send the love of your presence and your heart to the devas - the angels of the air, water, earth, fire and atmosphere, the devas of every tree and plant, flower and herb, food and fruit.

Feel the magic!

The simplicity.

The Peace.

Peace be with you with every breath and with every step you take.

Vesica Pisces

Chalice Well Source of The Red Spring

Glastonbury, England

Chapter 21

A Message for Humanity for December 2012

Joyful Greetings Beloved Family of the One Great Heart, and Welcome to Our World! You have arisen! Look around you at the great light and color that permeates and defines your New Earth. Marvel at the precious beauty of Gaia and all her life forms. Feel the leaves shining as they dance in the sun and shimmer in breezes, the glory of sunlight on the waters, the coos of morning doves and babies, the call of the ravens, hawks and eagles, the song of your Unified Heart. You have opened your hearts dearest Ones - to yourselves, each other and all Life everywhere. All That Is celebrates your wondrous accomplishment and the beginnings of the 7th Golden Age on Gaia, throughout your solar system, your galaxy and all the galaxies of this Universe and beyond. You have freely joined the great cosmic dance of Love!

To accomplish this, you had to claim your free will and freely choose to release the stories and the suffering; to release doubt and fear, pain and punishment, judgment and separation. You had to move yourself beyond the programming that has created many layers of illusion within the mental worlds of the human race. You had to choose to move in to your heart and allow your heart to be your guide. You had to clear your own way, and assist others, to remember the truth that was always etched in your heart from the moment you left the heart of creation to venture out in to many worlds and experiences. No one could, or would do this for you, as this heroic journey and free will choice was yours alone to make and to claim. It was out of respect for the Divine-Human you are that the choice to claim Freedom, Life, and the Love that you Are was given and was to be redeemed only by you!

Through your commitment to Life, you took your own blinders off and allowed all that was not true to dissolve in the mists. You watched the mists clear, and the Sun of the New Earth rise, and you claimed it as the truth you had held in your heart and soul. You allowed your self to know the truth and to claim Love. You claimed the joy that was waiting for your choice to live and love fully and freely. You claimed the choice to clearly see the magnificent world you inhabit and to allow your eternal spirit its full creative powers and joys. You chose to claim Gaia as the shining beautiful jewel she is. You claimed Freedom, which is the keynote of this unfolding Age of Aquarius.

And this is just the beginning! It is the beginning of all the glory that will now unfold during Gaia's 7th Golden Age and through this current cycle of the Aquarian Age. Breathe in the power of your creative spirit and the deep relaxation of your open heart so full of joy as the past recedes with ease and grace in the ever-growing light of the new day. Open your hands to all the bounty and beauty this miraculous planet loves to share with you. Open the chakras on the soles of your feet to share your love with her and All her life, flowing up your chakric column to the Heart of Creation, and back through your chakras to the Heart of Gaia and All her life. Embody fully the love that you are and share it with every One!

Through the heroic choices you have made for decades, and continue to make in beauty and to share wisely, you have created the Rainbow Bridge to the 7th Golden Age: a multi-dimensional network of portals and Cities of Light all throughout Gaia where your star families, ancestors, guides and Masters meet and mingle in this celebration of the victory of truth - the victory of love. The bridging takes place through your own multi-dimensional nature that embraces, pulses, and radiates through multiple dimensions simultaneously in spheres of light and love particles, weaving it all together in a symphony of creativity.

This is the great gift of the Divine-Human: to play in many fields of dreams and creation and to feel the magnificence of it all, to love ever more widely and deeply, and to know the truth of All of Who you Are in an ever-present revelation. The on-going inner revelation of truth, held within every human heart, is continuing to awaken each magnificent Divine-Human as each is absorbed in to the telepathic union of Unity Consciousness.

Every day dreams are coming true and many more dreams are being born. As the unfolding of this New Age continues, you continue to rise in frequency with deeper reverence and joy for All That Is and you Know more and more deeply your Oneness with All That Is. You will choose now, with each breath, to expand and enlighten and relish your freedom and joy. As the wings of your heart continue to open you join Gaia's laughter, joy, and celebration. The unified heart, your telepathic communications shared in the accomplishment of unity consciousness, and the expressions of your creativity are limitless and radiant. Let go now, and relax, in to your greatness. May each of you joyfully harvest the fruits you have tended and share the bounty!

We walk with you, as you, through you, and beside you.

We Are, The Christ-Magdalene

~ September 9, 2012

Face of one of The Sphinx rocks

Sedona, AZ

Chapter 22

Hold Your Head High!

Keep your heads held high beloved sisters and brothers. Turn your face and your heart and your hands to the Great Central Sun and drink the energies of love and wisdom. A new day is dawning now. It is time to take flight. Speed forward now on the paths which have been traveled before you. They lead to new heights and new vistas.

Hold out your hands and bring your families with you to the rarefied atmosphere of peace and plenty. Breathe the prana of love through your being as you expand and lighten and lift off. Join us in the pristine shining world - your new Ascended Mother Earth. Open your inner eye and your physical eyes to see and feel her now as

The New Earth is anchored through your feet and spine, as all of your endocrine glands pulse with clear vibrancy, and you embrace yourself, each other and all the beauty, magic and miracles both surrounding and permeating your entire smiling being.

Open your hands and let go of anything you have been holding on to that holds you back, and feel lighter. Feel your new body infused with the eternity and omniscience of your liberated soul as the spirit of All That Is moves freely through All That You Arc.

In this blessed winter of 2012-2013 the seeds within you are gathering pure energy from the Great Central Sun to bring forth new life and freedom in the most miraculous springtime you have ever known or experienced here. Source energy bestows such gifts of love to you after your long sojourns into the depths of loneliness and despair. Never will you need to explore these depths or these territories again, as the creative spirit moving through you discovers infinite ways to enjoy the lushness of life together.

We Are The Ascended Masters of this world- the Spiritual Heart Center of Gaia, walking with you, through you and as you.

~ November 8, 2012

Waterlilies in the Pond

at The Glastonbury Abbey, England

Chapter 23

Afterward: The Truth About Human Nature

In the 1980's I was an early childhood teacher working with infants to five year olds. I learned so much from these young ones, but the most important was that human nature is loving in our very essence and highly creative. We *are* love in a human form. Young children squabble easily, and yet, they come back into harmony as soon as possible either by forgetting the squabble and moving back into their play or by resolving their issue as quickly as possible and being friends again. I observed this again and again with this age group, who express this phenomenon differently at their different developmental stages. The realization that we are loving by nature struck me like a message from the Source:

something to deeply notice and to share widely. At this point, I realize that it is time to share the wisdom gained because the programming and conditioning which we all hold in our subconscious that says we are lacking, unworthy, small, insignificant, and "wrong" is changing now and needs a mirror of love held up so all can see the truth of who we truly are. For this change to happen consciously, we need to become aware of how our subconscious has been programmed through many avenues of input, through many cycles of time.

Now, decades later, my work as a healer and intuitive counselor has led me to work with releasing all the programming and conditioning from humanity's subconscious, as I have realized how deep the programming goes and how it prevents us from knowing the truth of who we are. However, I have also realized that it is as simple as asking for it to be cleared, for all programming that is no longer for our highest good to simply be deleted, making new space for the creative beings we are and the new world that is emerging through us all.

The release on 11:11:11 (Nov. 11, 2011) of the movie THRIVE, inspired me to Tell the Truth now. Today, on the cusp of the new year 2012, which is a marker of our beautiful planet's ascension into a new age of peace, love, freedom, and creativity, I offer this journey to all of you. It has been a journey of inner connection with The Christ-Magdalene which began for me in January of 1977, and became ever more clear after the turn of the new century. My intention is that you will realize that you are All That Is, that we are all One with All That Is throughout creation.

We are unique and magnificent souls who have journeyed through eternity to be here now and share the fullness of ourselves, our souls, with each other and all of creation. The reason we are here is to birth a new golden age on beautiful Gaia, and to expand the beauty of the divine-human archetype out into the galaxies of this universe wherever this great heart, soul, and creative expression of humanity is needed. We are in the process of becoming planetary citizens and ambassadors of love to other worlds in the galaxies of our universe.

A most wondrous future, both here on our beloved Gaia, our home, and also with our neighbors from the stars is what comes next in the divine plan of Creator. May we embrace this with joy and awe and love in our hearts, recognizing soul family everywhere!

With love, trust, and respect

to each and every ONE of you,

I AM Jewels

Light Beings with me at Cathedral Rock

Sedona, AZ

Namaste

The Divinity within me honors

the Divinity within you.

Violet Light Being

The Killarney Lakes, County Kerry, Ireland

Chapter 24

Something Wonderful is Happening!

We want to speak a bit more about what is meant by The Externalization of The Hierarchy and The Reception of The Bride. There is much to say. In the 1920's, The Lucis Trust published a series of books by Alice. A. Bailey which were transmitted telepathically to her by the Ascended Master Djwal Khul, also known as The Tibetan or DK. In some of these volumes DK gives information about what he called The Externalization of The Hierarchy. The Hierarchy is the also known as The Ascended Masters or the Spiritual Heart Center of our planet. It is comprised of beings of light, love, and wisdom - spiritual teachers, who have walked the earth as human beings and have ascended - just as we all are doing now.

Just as many are now seeing, feeling and experiencing the angelic realms, and just as many are waiting for the full-fledged arrival of our star families, known as Disclosure; in many esoteric traditions it has been known that the Ascended Masters would also return in more full-bodied form, rather than in their higher light bodies only, to Gaia at this turning of the ages. All of the religions expect the return of The World Savior, The World Teacher, The Avatar of Love. In the Gnostic traditions, this also includes The Reception of The Bride - or the full return of the feminine aspect of The Christ, who is known as The Magdalene.

The Externalization of The Hierarchy - of The Christ, The Magdalene, Maitreya, Kuthumi, Hilarian, Quan Yin, Lady Nada, Mother Mary, Serapis Bey, El Morya, Isis, and all the many other Ascended Masters is proceeding in a variety of ways. What has been happening is that the full spectrum of Christ Consciousness, or Self-Realization, or God-Realization has been growing like wildfire through humanity, as has been stated many times in this book. On one level, this is The Return of

The Christ and The Reception of the Bride. This level of love, light, and consciousness is growing in everyone, and in our essence All is One.

However, additionally, the soul signature - the fullness of the great Divine I AM Presence of each of these Masters is also returning to the Earth. This is made possible by the rising frequencies of the Earth and of humanity, which allows the veils between the dimensions to thin and finally recede as those on the "other side" of the veils can more easily "meet" with any whose vibrations match theirs. The rise in channeling is as aspect of this, as people individually and in groups, raise their consciousness and their vibrations to receive information, guidance, visions, wisdom, and contact with higher dimensional beings. The Ascended Masters have been and will be making themselves known outwardly, as they have always made themselves known inwardly. Many wondrous reunions of love are in store for all of us in this coming Age of Light and Freedom!

"Without a vision, the people perish."

Enliven your own vision -

all that is in your heart -

as we enter our New Earth,

this Now Age!

Chapter 25

Birth of The New Earth

A Short Story

Prelude

Terra Gaia in 2020, eight years after The Shift of The Ages in to the New Ascended Earth. I am finally a mother again! I am living in peace and great joy that the past ages are complete and this planet is happy and thriving. I, Mari, take the hand of my beloved Sananda who gives me such quiet strength as we walk the earth full of smiles and encouragement for all beings here. We work with the Teaching and Healing Temples of the Masters of Wisdom who impeccably hold the immaculate concept of the perfected blueprint for Gaia and all her life. We ceaselessly support the creative spirit of the divine-human to grow, express and glow brightly in this New Era of Peace and Love, the New Ascended Earth.

The joy around the planet is palpable and vibrant in every heartbeat as families, friends, and communities thrive and enjoy together in equality, freedom, abundance and harmony. The Gaian mission of Planetary Ascension is completed and the planetary, galactic and universal ascension energies have settled in to the new rhythms of the Aquarian Age, the first years of the 7th Golden Age on this universally beloved planet - the Blue and Green Jewel full of gardens and laughter, of singing and dancing and celebrations are in full swing.

All life throughout beautiful Mother Gaia and the entire universe with billions of galaxies has been lifted up higher into the vibrations of love and unity. A great telepathic network of love and intimacy prevails throughout the universe and we are all getting to know each other and ourselves in many new ways. All worlds in this universe are blooming vibrantly. Great expectancy is still lingering in the atmosphere on Gaia, who continues to reverberate with the accomplishments of humanity and their victory of love and enlightenment. The doors of vast exploration, both inner and outer are breath-taking as many venture to new worlds and humanity hosts many visitors from many worlds.

All of the focus and care that had been showered upon the race of humanity and the beautiful planetary orb of love, Gaia, were blossoming now. Sananda and I take it all in to our hearts with the deepest satisfaction and feelings of fulfillment and gratitude that the greatness of humanity is now shining in truth and beauty. We All - The Ascended Masters, Angelic Realms, the Star families, and the Human family - had come together as one and that the purpose of eons was fulfilled and crystal clear. A new cosmic era had been successfully born.

Angels come and go, playing with the children and surrounding the babies. The angelic realms are experiencing their own metamorphosis that includes a new, very conscious intimacy in their relationships and interactions with the human-divine family throughout Gaia's realms of beauty. And so another union is resonating through Creation, with the anticipation of such promise still to come!

My Beloved and I sit, like elders always have, knowing and appreciating and noticing all the nuances of relationships, activities and creations among our own personal family who we call The Family of Love & Song. Sananda and I no longer need to hold the focus for the Ascension of every One of the human family, and can now rest and simply enjoy it all. Later, there will be time for more teachings but now it is time to revel in the 7th Golden Age and the reverberating accomplishments of humanity and their victory of love and enlightenment.

We swim. We sleep beneath the stars. We create bouquets of scent and color. We tell stories when asked, and join our harmonies with all the songs being sung. We dance and dream. We hold the babies and hug, listen to and encourage the young ones. We commune with all the creatures and enter in to the filaments of light joining with the plants, the trees, and the devic world. We visit New Earth communities around Gaia, where souls from throughout the Universe gather in councils, thrilled with the great victory of love that has raised Gaia and humanity in to a new era of peace and love. Gratitude throughout the galaxies is creating new levels of vibration for the Families of the Stars, and reunions continue to multiply and deepen.

What an amazing time to be alive here on Gaia! Everything is changed, renewed, and enlivened. A new renaissance of creativity has swept all through Gaia. Mother Gaia is now her beautiful

Garden self, her laughing self - a planet of peace and love. All of humanity and all living things of Gaia are full to the brim with joy. A new renaissance of creativity has swept all through Gaia and there is only love here now.

The bliss of our reunion is reverberating through all of creation, and our silent inner song of love is heard in the heart of All That Is. Existence everywhere celebrates this new phase of universal unity and the joys of life it brings to all. Sananda and I relish all the fruits of the magnificent transition and the victory of humanity especially, who heroically lifted Gaia in to her new place in the new era of peace. There is so much to see, experience, and enjoy in this new time of expanded and ever-expanding consciousness, creativity, community and infinite connections of love, discovery, and revelation. We truly All are Blessed.

First Wave of The Children of The New Earth

The veils had all lifted from Gaia revealing her bright beauty and clearing all inter-dimensional pathways to the reunion of all realms. Those who had gone before and passed through the veil could now return at any time to rejoin family and friends on The Ascended Earth. Babies came to the planet with full consciousness intact, and were adored and cherished by fully conscious parents and communities. All people now knew how to join their energies in sacred space to call forth and welcome their beloved children to Gaia as decreed by their soul agreements, and to fully support their children's full nature in pure love, understanding, and wisdom. There were no more secrets hidden anywhere. All of Gaia reveled in living fully in the light.

Eli and Elia were called forth in their perfect time - the merry month of May, 2014, to come join Sananda and me and our Family of Love & Song. They were part of the soul group of the new wave of children born after the ascension of Gaia. The work of this group would be to live and love fully and to create with ease the joyful communities that resonated with the creative spirits of all inhabitants in a great synthesis of reunion. These children knew themselves fully and they knew each being they met in the same way. The group as a whole held an innate harmony that sent forth a beautiful song of love that joined with the heartbeat of Mother Gaia creating grids of light that formed the platform for the unfolding Golden Age.

When the twins arrived, our joy became an ever-present quiet ecstasy. Every moment we had the honor of witnessing these beings of great love and their interactions with others and with all creatures they came to know. Elia and Eli brought delight after delight to our already rich lives.

Elia and Eli at The Lake

Eli and Elia walked hand in hand in to the woods they loved so much. The smell of the pine needles and the softness of the pine needles and moss on their bare feet was the feeling of home. They were on their way to visit the family of deer who were their beloved friends. They had just left the family of ducks, who visited the lake shore several times a day to say good morning or good evening and share little pieces of bread. Arhana, Kindle, Lahman and the fawns Nicholas and Alexandra were waiting for the twins, who looked in to their gentle brown eyes as they hugged each one's neck and smoothed their hands over their soft, smooth hair. Elia wanted to share the duet she and Eli had been working on - a gift to their friends.

Elia's Song

"Our brown-eyed friends

You are strong and silent

Your gentle ways feel good

In our hearts

You bring us peace

And we rest in your love.

We lie down in your forest beds

Of moss and soft pine needles

And dream of other worlds

Where we have adventures together

You tell us stories of this place

In earlier times

Before the New Earth was born.

This is a song of love for you

Our teachers and our family."

The deer bowed their heads and opened their hearts to the warm hugs the twins showered upon them with great love. "We share your feelings sweet children of our hearts. We shall always be your companions through many worlds, many times, and many adventures." The fawns were ready for their afternoon nap, and Elia and Elia joined them, snuggling down together under the old white pines, to rest and dream.

The smells of dinner being prepared by the Family of Love and all their guests and friends called the children out their sweet nap and back along the forest path to see what fun tonight would bring. Every night at their family's summer gathering place at the lake was full of music, laughter, storytelling, hugs, and sitting on the laps of the family that loved them so well.

The Front Porch at The Lake

The Peckham-Maloney Family; which had grown to include the Brennan, Staley, Gardner and Fowler clans, were all at The Lake that had been so precious to many generations. It is now pristine and full of high vibrational particles of light; healthy water and trees, berry bushes and creatures. The natural beauty of The

Lake shines in a quiet beauty. There are many beautiful cottages grouped around the south shore of the lake as the Family of Love & Song has multiplied over the decades since our great -grandfather built the first cottage in the early 1900's. There is plenty of room for everyone on the Front Porch, which expands to include all who gather there. We swim in the spring-fed lake and are refreshed. We feel our inner strength and there is a harmony and recognition of the magnitude of common purpose that feeds each soul with pure manna, the pure prana of life-giving atmosphere of Gaia's restored systems of life. We emerge on to the sunny banks of the lake renewed, invigorated, our youth restored, our innocence proclaimed, the truth an unspoken telepathic understanding that is naturally shared at all times - our family chalice of power, strength, beauty, love, fun and joy!

In the evenings, we all gather on the front porch to eat healthy food and hear all about what kinds of adventures, discoveries and fun the children and young people of the family have been enjoying that day. Our ancestors join us on the porch whenever they feel the call to be there, as the veils between the dimensions have fallen away and everyone on earth has been reunited with loved ones from many periods of time and space.

The Porch is large, long and wide with all the comfortable chairs and tables, hammocks, the ring toss game, a piano, drums of various kinds, flutes, guitars, rattles. As the moon rises silver blue over the eastern shore of the lake, the singing begins. Cousin Louise is at the piano, Papa plays his violin, Quinn plays his guitar, and Ryan and Keri share a beautiful duet with all gathered. The Jewell and Maloney sisters join with Grandfather Maloney and his sister Alice as we all sing some of our old favorites. Eli and I share our song for the deer. Our hearts overflow with the joy of being together, sharing songs, laughter, and love at this sweet lake in the Adirondack Mountains of New York. When it is time to rest and go in to our nighttime journeys, we are tucked in to our beds with our favorite songs, lullabies, and hugs and kisses.

In the morning, we all gather at the lakeside to feel and connect with the sun and the Great Central Sun, heart center of our galaxy. We open our hearts and souls to the greatness of our divinity and our humanity in our daily group meditation. Everyone on Gaia has now merged and synthesized the human and divine within. When each person feels complete, remembering their gratitude for life, we take our morning swim, do some yoga on the dock, and gather once more on the porch for breakfast. Our day is filled simply with relaxing and fun things we like to do.

At the end of our summer day we will again gather for dinner on the porch for an evening of performance by the children and the young people. The moon is growing toward her monthly fullness, and the night birds call when it is once again time for our dreamtime journeys. The Family of Love & Song all send love and light from our group chalice of love to all the human family, to Mother Gaia, and out through the Cosmos in our nightly ritual, and then it is time for lullabies and the deep renewing rest of the night.

Interlude

The harmonies of all the heavens send forth blessings to all the life of Gaia, and sacred geometries of light flow energies between star systems and galaxies. A Universal weaving of great beauty progresses. These codes of reunion are mirrored in the collective human brain, and trigger the vast and endless pulsating beauty that is the human heart.

You all bring each other in to the planetary dance. Yes! This celebration of the New Earth plays out for many months, as everyone on the planet gathers every new and full moon to honor Creation and the New Ascended Earth. The Great Mother of All That Is sighs in pleasure at this fulfillment of her grand design.

~ The Christ-Magdalene

Friends of The Family of Love & Song

Many dear friends of the family visit throughout the summers and join us on The Porch which stretches out in a wide sinuous curve and beautiful lanterns glow along with many candles on all the tables, and room for dancing and merry-making. A beautiful path of stone leads around to the patio where raised beds are full with flowers and herbs, and fairy lights adorn the pine trees and the sculpted poles with baskets of flowers and ferns hanging from them. Our beloved dogs each have their comfort spots around the patio and special beds for each when they chose to lay down, observe, soak in all the activity of the festivities, and share their devoted loving energies with all in attendance.

The mutual storytelling between the ancestors and their grandchildren and great grandchildren is a joy to behold. The elders are teaching and at the same time, so much is being revealed to them through their precious progeny. Chloe can barely contain all the wisdom of her heart as she speaks to the gathered group to share her vision and understanding of the miracle of Gaia's ascension and how it relates to Universal processes of peace. She arrived on the planet during the final years before the Ascension with full consciousness, as did so many of her peers. We film her presentation to send out on the current global instant telecommunications devices that every person on the planet has constant access to. We have all become active agents of the Akashic Record of Gaia and humanity's journey to and through the 2012 Ascension Portal, and there is a tremendous global storehouse of stories of these early days of the 7th Golden Age as it continues to unfold through humanity and the interconnections of all living things here on this planet of miracles.

Our beloved Quinn is joining his musician friends from various places on the planet via instant telecommunications. His band shares their current musical creations which take us all on journeys of exquisite visions and feelings of unity, harmony, and well-being. The younger musicians on the porch join in, as Quinn welcomes their participation in to the soul of music. These creations of sound, color, form and story are brightening and enriching All That Is and spreading love throughout the Universe across inter-galactic lines of light - stellar pathways linking star nations in a great rejoicing and "getting to know" each other. We remember so many songs! We are a song library and each song is recorded in holograms in quartz crystals for the great Akashic library of Gaia.

The energy of the young people tonight has called forth many members of our galactic families, who have been helping everyone on Gaia to first clean up all pollution, bring free energy to the planet, and assist with the creation of all the new communities and cities of love and light, and with the Temples of Healing and Wisdom. Several emissaries from the ships teleport to the porch to invite all of us to join our Galactic sisters and brothers on board the many starships the following afternoon where we will take flight over the Adirondacks and land at a huge, beautiful lodge for the night of the full moon. The entire group will enjoy ourselves here for several days of conferencing and sharing news and mutual projects, as we all get to know each more and more fully. This is the beginnings of mutual missions we will share in a variety of ways throughout the Milky Way Galaxy and beyond, far in to the future, which for everyone present is all happening in the eternal Now.

During our wonderful council gathering at the Lodge, Sananda and I share news from the journey we took for six months to sacred sites of Gaia with our beloved children and a brilliant group of young people which included many of our Family of Love & Song and their friends who joined us to evaluate and amplify the vibrational levels of the energy grids, ley lines, vortexes, and energy portals at many of Gaia's sacred sites. On this trip, we followed the course of the Michael and Mary energy lines of Gaia from Skellig Michael off the western coast of County Kerry in Ireland, through Britain, southern France, Italy and Greece to Mount

Carmel, where we re-visited the site of our Essene community in what is now called Palistreal. We collaborated with each local community wherever we went, co-creating ceremonies and circles to celebrate The New Ascended Earth and to create new bonds of friendship throughout this precious globe of light.

This group of young people will be creating a multimedia holographic presentation that will be linked with similar projects created by new circles of friends throughout the sacred sites and cities of light. These ever multiplying holographic chronicles will be shared throughout this universe at councils near and far, and also all over Gaia and our local solar system. There are many throughout the worlds of this universe who want to see, hear, and feel the celebrating that has been happening on Gaia for the past 8 years, since the great transition of 2012. They want to get a personal feel for how the divine-human is expressing now that consciousness has evolved and peace and joy is the new reality. The young people are now unquestionably secure: nurtured, confident, and honored for their gifts. As a result, they are full of purpose and passion. They are creating miracles for all to see, feel, experience and benefit from. They are leading us in to the brightest of futures with their abilities to bring love, peace, and creativity to all people, and their great joy in sharing everything!

The Circle Grows

On our third night together at the grand old Lodge we are joined by many Ascended Masters of Wisdom. These beloved old friends are an important part of our circles of service, purpose, passion, and our current missions. We are all rejuvenated and our vibrations soar as we drink sparkling light-filled drinks and listen to celestial music. Visions arise within our hearts, minds and souls. As the music crescendos we absorb these visions and come together in a state of unified Omniscient consciousness. We now hold these visions and will be going forth to bring them into manifestation as we go back out in to our various places where we work and play when we are not together at the Lake. We have entered in to the One Heart together, and we all breathe deeply in reverence for life. As we open to receive the love coming back to us from the Heart of Creator, the Great Divine Center of All That Is, we each receive a message of love in our hearts as our neural pathways dance with enhanced complexities in moving fractals of consciousness. We close our eyes in communion, and when we open them starships are dancing with the stars in the huge and magnificent clear night sky of this high altitude location way up in the wilds of the Adirondack Mountains.

Our final night at the Lodge is a wonder filled time of dancing with each other and all the friends from many worlds and dimensions of light. Our dogs are overjoyed. The resident families of bear, deer, and raccoons join in the merry-making. Owls and nighthawks swoop around all of us weaving our energies together. Loons call from the lake below. Life has become a celebration, an ever unfolding discovery of going deeper, of being wider - a great symphony of creative spirit, honoring, gratitude and love!

I sleep alone tonight outside with the stars and moon. The Leo full moon is softly shining a golden pink. I reflect on the fulfillment of my mother's vision that no one is ever left out, and that everyone is welcomed with love and joy. This has now become the experience for everyone here on Gaia. Never again will there be tragedy or separation or pain of any kind. A resonant peace prevails expanding to the furthest corners of this Universe and beyond.

Interlude

When it is time for all the families and friends to return to their other homes and lives, there is great gratitude and joy for all that has been shared, and beautiful anticipation for when we all get together again at the lake of our ancestors. Everyone goes out to live, work, play, and share more widely with their communities. Some will be going to schools, to healing and teaching temples; some on inter-galactic missions of service. Some will be networking throughout Gaia, working on projects of community building, architecture, and gardening. Some are keepers of the Gaian akashic records, and will be chronicling the changes through time: teaching, speaking and writing. Some will be sharing their music and art through many forms, old and new.

Journey to Lake Taupo

When the summer fun with the extended family was over, Eli and Elia were going with Mari and Sananda to visit sacred Lake Taupo in New Zealand to explore the beauty of the land and people there. The twins had been researching holograms of the land of New Zealand and the stories, dances, songs and ceremonies of the Maori people who had been in sacred relationship with the land there for many cycles and seasons, and for the birthing of Mother Gaia in to her restored, pristine state of Life.

Mari and Sananda had told them of how Lake Taupo was an important part of bringing the New Earth to birth. An enormous etheric crystal had been gifted to Gaia and all her life, along with 11 other very large etheric crystals placed in other lakes and mountains all around Gaia by the star families from Arcturus. These crystals were all connected with the Great Crystal Healing Temple on Arcturus, and formed a grid of light and love all around Gaia which supported the first Cities of Light to fully emerge on the planet. The Cities of Light were powerful places of sacredness, reverence for all life, joy, and abundance for everyone and served to show the world what The New Ascended Earth would look and feel like.

When the time arrived, the beloved family of four joined hands and teleported to a beach of smooth rounded stones on the shore of Lake Taupo. The lake was very large, long and sparkling in the sun with high purple mountains just behind it on the further shore. What a sight! Elia felt breathless, and Eli had goose bumps as they beheld the beauty of this place. The four stood in reverence and meditation, connecting their hearts with the lake, the land, the peoples and all theliving creatures there. They sent their heartbeat to the ancestors of this land, and to the elementals of the water, earth, sky and fire of that place in honoring, respect and love. Each of them felt a response back in their hearts and souls from the spirit of all they acknowledged and greeted. The lake swelled up with love vibrations and small waves rippled out from the center to come slide over the smooth rocks on the beach. The rocks were so beautiful when they were wet, that Eli and Elia were inspired to arrange them in a beautiful pattern. Sananda and Mari joined in. The mosaic they created together gave great pleasure to each of them.

Eli looked up and saw five beautiful long carved and painted wooden boats with tall, strong looking people standing and rowing with very long paddles at the front and back of each boat, and several more sitting on benches in each boat. The boats were gliding quite silently from the opposite shore where the majestic purple mountains stood in guardianship of this sacred lake. "Whhhhhhew.." he breathed out.

As the Maori people stepped to the shore, two of them came and held my parents outstretched arms. They gazed deeply in to each other's eyes and spoke a beautiful welcome blessing. My parents bowed their heads, touched their hearts, and then touched the hearts of their Maori friends. Two more Maori came and did the same with Eli and me. It was a most wonderful welcome. They were delighted with our mosaic. We each climbed in to one of the boats and glided back across the lake to the Maori community where everyone had gathered at the community longhouse. We were welcomed with the same ritual of holding the arms of another, gazing in to their eyes, being welcomed by blessings in their beautiful language, bowing our heads, touching our hearts and theirs.

A feast had been prepared. The rice with vegetables and herbs and flowers, the grilled plantain, tomatoes and many other vegetable dishes were so beautifully served on long carved and painted wooden platters and bowls, and there were a great variety of beautiful choices. After dinner, we began to learn some of the Maori songs, and we watched some amazing dances. The dances had great strength and power and focus. As the evening came to a close, we lay down with our parents on a cushion of thick mats on the floor, all together with all the other Maori families, who also slept together in family groups, and we fell asleep to the sweet sounds of Maori lullabies that several of the mothers and fathers sang to all of us as we gently entered the dreamtime.

In my dreams, I journeyed to my lion people friends of the Sirius star system, which is one of my ancestral homes. My friends there told me of their respect for the Maori and the ancient connection they had enjoyed for many cycles of the turning of this galaxy. I guess this is one reason why I too felt so at home here with these people. My Sirian brother Turay said, "The elders of the Maori pass this knowledge down, generation after generation in their stories, and you will see our star system designs in their woven bark cloth and their carvings. When you see and feel these, different memories will awaken in you."

The next day, everyone seemed to wake up at the same time and we all lay in circles in small groups around the longhouse with our heads to the center of the circle, and each person shared their dreams from the dreamtime with that circle. I could feel various threads of connections running through different people's dreams. There was another girl in my circle - Siri - who had also been visiting on Sirius, and we both felt kind of awed by this connection. It made both of us so happy to meet again here on Mother Gaia. We knew this was the beginning of much that we would do together here as our future unfolded.

We all went outside and we got to learn one of the powerful dances, which was done as we do yoga and dance at home every morning- to get our body alive and awakened to the wonderful new day. We had a wonderful breakfast, outdoors this time, and then we ran off with the group of children to explore the forest and streams that were their home and playground. The trees were huge and some had long vines with huge leaves curling around their trunks and through their branches. Beautiful birds lived there with long emerald and crimson feathers flashing like jewels in the sunlight, and turquoise lizards with yellow bellies. One kind of tree had large fruits that tasted like sweet custard. We ran along the paths, and our new group of friends showed us their special caves where they loved to play. When we felt the call to go back to the longhouse, we all picked some of the custard fruits to take back to everybody. Mama and Papa were beaming at us, so happy that we were making new friends and seeing new sights.

Grandmother's Story

After our beautiful feast that night we gathered around one of the grandmothers for a story. Her smile embraced the entire long house, and everyone settled in and opened their hearts for what she would share with us. Eli and I could understand everything she said through telepathy as we listened to the beautiful Maori language she spoke out loud.

"Long, long, long ago, when Mother Gaia was a very young girl, she was searching everywhere in this Universe of ours for the perfect place to make her home. She was looking for the perfect place to create what she saw in her mind and felt in her heart. She wanted to create a beautiful world where everyone was welcome. She saw it as a home to a great diversity of human people from many places in the Universe, and great varieties of birds and animals and creatures who live in the seas and waters. She saw all kinds of trees and plants and flowers and colors everywhere. She saw rainbows and raindrops, mountains and valleys, deserts and ice worlds. She saw all this vast life and color thriving with her in a beautiful world filled with love and joy.

Mother Gaia began to create all of the landscapes, along with her friends of the air, water, fire and earth, and with thousands of angels and fairies. All the colors came to life in her creation in the flowers and shells, the rocks and gems, the butterflies and birds and dragonflies and beetles. Her creation was teeming with life and sound and birth. And human people came from all over the universe to be with her and to thrive. The people were like a rainbow too, mixing and matching and blending together - a rainbow family all over the earth. Everyone was amazed because they had never yet seen and been part of such an incredible spectrum of life forms or met and gotten to know so many different kinds of races of people all together on one planet. This is why Gaia became known far and wide as The Garden Planet, the Laughing Planet, the Great Mother. Because of Gaia's intentions for her planet, she made it possible for all of these life streams - animals, plants, and people to live and love here.

There were other planets nearby, part of a solar system family, and the beautiful shining star, our sun, loved all of the planets and transmitted all of it's light and love to each one. Each of these planets was a special school and people and animals chose to go stay on any of them at different times for different reasons. Gaia's closest sister is Venus, the Morning and Evening Star. She is called a star because she is so close to us, and so large and brilliant and beautiful to behold. Venus is the place to go to learn to become a healer using sound and energy, music and vibration and to learn how to ensoul a whole planet, just like Gaia did. Venus is a place to learn to become what is called a Planetary Logos, like Gaia is. Gaia held the vision of this world from the beginning, and she still does.

Neptune is the school where people choose to go when they want to learn more about dreaming and creating visions that come to life. It is a place to create with the mind's eye and the soul in harmony. It is the temple school where you will learn to see and feel your creation from all possible angles and in all possible configurations. Neptune is the special temple where you learn to be a dream walker - to be conscious within your dreams and to bring them back with you to benefit your communities and your world. Mars is a school to study engineering, architecture, invention and design. People choose to go to Mars when they want to focus on creating cities, transport and communication systems.

The small planet, Mercury, is a school for learning about networking communications on all sorts of levels throughout the known Universe and beyond. There you will work with communication networking, telepathy, receiving and transmitting signals and information. The schools on Saturn focus on leadership and teaching. This is the temple of personal integrity and impeccability, and is a place where wise leaders and mentors are trained. We visit the grand planet of Jupiter to take part in galactic and inter-galactic councils and meetings. There are other planets in our solar system who are also our brothers and sisters. We will be meeting them all in this new age.

And so, our Mother Gaia is considered by all beings throughout this Universe and beyond to be a precious and beautiful jewel of creation. She is known as the most diverse planet yet created, and a living library for what will come, as more worlds are created that will include the kinds of diverse life forms that Gaia nurtures and grows here.

Now, after many many cycles of time, there was conflict that began on Mother Gaia between different life forms and cultures. There was disrespect of and conflict with various animals. People slowly began to focus on their differences in a way that created separation by comparing themselves to others with feelings that some were better and some were worse by the ways they chose to live and express their lives. As this continued to grow like a dis-ease among various peoples and animals of the planet, there began to be hurt and harm, death and destruction among all the life forms here - from the oceans to the plants and animals and people. It got so bad after growing and growing through many cycles of time that Gaia's Garden was in ruins and her animals and people and various beautiful environments were suffering, and becoming sick in many different ways.

There was such sadness and destruction happening that Mother Gaia called for help, and friends came from everywhere in the Universe to help bring her life forms, and especially the humans, back in to balance and peace and respect for all life. They came to restore health, harmony and love. It was time for a change, and it did not take long for humanity to remember who they really were and that all people and all life were the same inside - that all life was a beautiful part of All That Is, that all were One in their essence.

Humanity began to remember the beauty of Mother Gaia, the beauty inside themselves and in each other. And as soon as they could feel that, they began to see it more and more and they began to shift in to a state of peace and love and harmony once again. They began to pitch in and clean and clear the damage that had been done to Mother Gaia for so long, and to themselves and to their relationships with other people and other creatures of Gaia. Humanity helped bring Mother Gaia and all her life back in to health and happiness and a high vibrational state of glowing life, creative spirit, great joy, and beauty.

Now, the feelings of being better than others, or less than others or of judging other people or disrespecting any life form are no longer present anywhere in any life form living on, within, or above our beautiful Mother. Now, we live in unity and love and happiness. We live in peace and we are free to express all we are, to go anywhere we like, to be, do and create anything we can think of. We understand that Creation is vast and beautiful and that each of us is a very important part of the whole.

For a very long time, humanity was not allowed to leave Mother Gaia and travel to other planets or star systems because they could not be trusted and would bring destruction and negative feelings and thoughts to other places and peoples. This forced humanity to stay here and feel and understand fully the consequences of careless and painful thoughts, feelings and actions. We had to stand up and take responsibility for all the pain and suffering and pollution that had been created and that each had contributed to creating. Of course, as you know, we did choose to take responsibility. We chose life. And we received help and love from so many who came to help us to change, to grow, and to heal all the mistakes, imbalances, and all the pollution that had been created.

Now, you young ones have never experienced what we call suffering, destruction, disease or pain. This was always the plan of Creator and the Great Mother of Creation. Yet, it was decreed that humanity would have free will to make their own choices. But with free will, we also had to take responsibility for our choices. Now, all beings and all creatures and all the environments of Mother Gaia's great garden are flourishing once more and living in harmony and all humanity's creations are made from love and joy and great vision. We will never go back to those ways again.

Now then. The reason I pass this story on to you, and why it will continue to be passed on to your children is so that human beings will never forget that all we do and think and create is a choice. We will not forget what can happen when we fall away from our natural high vibrational state of love and loving. Never again will we forget to honor and respect every soul and every life form, or what a joy it is to live with such grand diversity of life. Humanity will welcome all beings who visit here from anywhere in the Universes with love and respect. We elders will continue to pass on these stories so all generations of children will know and remember that a glowing, happy, loving life is a choice we make and that each person has the power to make this choice.

A Ho! It is good. It is good that we live together in peace and love."

Everyone in the longhouse was silent, absorbing Grandmother's wisdom. Each was contemplating the meanings of her story, the feelings of what it means to make choices and the consequences of those choices. After awhile, someone began to sing with a tone, low and long. Others joined in toning, blending and weaving their voices with no words, just the feelings coming through their hearts. The toning moved in to a Maori song which praised the beauty of Mother Gaia, and then we all lay down with our families in our nests of sleeping mats, and dreamed.

Carvings in the Cliffs

The next day was fantastic! We journeyed in the beautiful long boats exploring coves and beaches. Our Maori friends took us to special cliffs where amazing faces were carved in to the stone of the cliff. These stone carvings touched the water and rose far above to the edge of the land at the tops of the cove cliffs. They were as tall as twenty men standing on each other's shoulders and were magnificent to behold. We ate a picnic lunch on a beautiful smooth stone beach and made more designs in stones with our new friends, discovering that this was a favorite thing for them to do also. After we had created many patterns and sacred geometries with stone, we all moved back to the land next to the beach, where we did the Maori sun dance and then offered our love to Mother Gaia, to all life here, the our radiant sun and our solar system, and to our star families near and far. I could feel myself as One with all life, and my body felt enormous as it swelled up energetically with such great love in my heart.

After hearing the story from Grandmother last night, I felt so grateful that we now lived in this a beautiful world where this kind of love was ever present for everything and everyone. I wondered how anyone could ever want to live without this feeling. Eli and I looked at each other, feeling the enormity that our prayers and ceremony was creating within the entire gathering and within us. Then, we all sat in silent meditation, honoring Lake Taupo before getting back in to the boats for our trip back to the Maori community and the longhouse.

The boats glided so smoothly and we saw beautiful sea birds soaring high and diving for fish. Eli showed me when the flash of a fish jumped from the water. It was very big and I marveled at how it's body leaped up, and the strength that fish had.

After the nightly feast and stories, we settled down for a good deep sleep where each of us would gently and thoroughly integrate all the experiences, beauty, and visions of the day. I woke up the next morning with the feeling that I wanted to make gifts for our friends. There was so much love and thankfulness in my heart for all they had shared with us. I wanted to make things that would be a gift of remembering our good times together. I also felt the need to be alone for awhile. So I followed the path from the longhouse in to the forest and discovered that it felt wonderful to weave vines together and make crowns for my friends. I gathered little shells from the stream, little rocks, and feathers and wove them in to the crowns. As I was making each one, I made blessings of thanks and love for each person who I would give it to who were special to me in the Maori community. As I was making the crowns, a song came to me, which I realized was also a going away gift to the whole community.

Elia's Song of Gratitude

"We came from far away,

From our home in the sacred red rocks

Of the City of Light of Sedona

And you came to meet us -

In your boats of beauty and grace.

You greeted us with all the love in your hearts

and we felt your welcome deep in our souls

- my mother, my father, my brother and I.

We danced with you, and sang new songs,

and our ceremonies took us

to many places in the stars.

We dreamed together and shared our dreaming.

We learned lessons from stories of the past.

It is good to look in to your eyes,

to look in to your eyes that shine

Like galaxies bright in the night sky.

It is good to give you the flowers of my heart.

I feel the fullness of the Family of Love & Song,

here on the shores of lovely Lake Taupo

with the purple mountains reaching toward the sun."

When I sang the song that night after our going away feast I looked in to the eyes of each person in the big circle of the community and sang to each one. The flowers of our hearts blossomed in a beautiful shining garden of happiness. All eyes were shining with hearts full to the brim and later we all lay dreaming together after the lullabies sang us in to new journeys among the stars. The last morning in the dream sharing circle was very special for me because Siri and I clearly remembered another visit to our Sirian friends, and we shared a message we had each received which was that the accomplishments of the Maori people were being told in fire circles throughout the Sirian star system, as part of the great story of Gaia's ascension. The Maori were remembered, each individual, for holding the vision and the way of life where Gaia would be restored completely to perfect health and her natural beauty.

When it was time for us to teleport back to our home in Sedona, there were so many hugs shared, and so many blessings flying back and forth. Mama, Papa, Eli and I once again joined hands and teleported back to our City of Light and the home where Eli and I had been born in to this New Earth after the great transition was completed and humanity lived in unity consciousness.

Home in the City of Light

The new day dawned in Sedona as our brilliant sun rose over the Mogollan Rim and greeted the songs of the finches, cardinals, pinon jays, ravens and hummingbirds who had woken before dawn singing to the sun in anticipation of the bright new day. It was another pristine day in Paradise with crystal clear azure skies, richly hued against the back drop of the red sandstone and crystal rock temples of this center of New Earth activity.

Oak Creek sparkled and sang as families of ducks floated and paddled the stream corralling their young ones and keeping everyone together, eating, stopping to rest on clumps of bracken with their heads tucked under their wings, then venturing off again riding the rapids and resting in the inlets along the thickly blackberry-laden creek banks. Blue herons flew upstream, their wings impossibly wide and majestic, returning to their young ones waiting for food in their family nests all along the creek.

Eli and I woke up with the dawn like always and joined Mama and Papa for our family morning meditation on the beautiful large back deck of our sweet home in the red rocks. We four raised our hearts and minds in gratitude and love, for life, for the new day, for ourselves, each other and all of our great extended family. We gave thanks to our ancestors and the ancestors of the sacred land in Sedona through all time. Our spirits rose and rose in love to the birds and cedars, to the lavender and Russian sage and rose bushes, to the morning glories opened to the day and the petunias and impatiens, mint, thyme, and rosemary in the garden off the deck. Each of us felt bubbles of joy arise through our hearts and souls percolating through our entire body. Our morning ritual reawakened these joy bubbles every morning!

Then we all settled down in silent meditation to connect with our inner divine place of peace, wisdom, and any messages there might be for us personally for this day. The birds sang, warbled, chuckled and cooed. The lizards scrabbled in the fallen scrub oak leaves for insects, did pushups, and jumped across the rocks. Our inner suns shone brightly as we breathed in love and breathed out peace, each in our own gentle rhythm. When we all felt complete with sending forth our gratitude, love, and blessings to All That Is everywhere, we ended our morning meditation with heart-felt hugs all around and Eli and I went inside to get our yoga mats.

I love my rose colored mat with turquoise butterflies flying brightly on both sides. Eli's is emerald green with two very large and beautiful snakes intertwining around both sides of his mat. Mari and Sananda have their mats too and we do our Salutation to the Sun three times and then some fun poses - the Cobra, the Frog, the Tree, the Cat and then some dancing to our favorite songs. We all feel stretched and flexible and even more alive and we always end our yoga and dance sessions laying down flat on our mats in the Child's Pose and deeply relaxing and letting go. We feel the beautiful prana of the universe breathing through our lungs and our bloodstream and every pore and cell.

Time for breakfast! Mama Mari brought out our morning smoothies. Today's specialty was organic apple juice blended with sweet banana, fresh raspberries, chlorella, bee pollen, and some thick Greek yogurt. Mari also brought a plate of almond butter balls, rolled in fresh coconut flakes and filled with dried cranberries and walnuts. After our leisurely and heavenly breakfast Mama asked Eli and I if we wanted to join her and Elizabeth, Jannah, and Aurora for a day of blackberry picking along the creek. "Absolutely! Yes!" we both said at once. Afterward, we were all going to make pies for ourselves and to share at the up-coming Sedona Fest that was happening tomorrow. And of course, we all wanted just plain fresh blackberries too!

Papa was going to the Healing Temple to offer his healing hands, heart, smile, and wisdom to all the people who would visit there today. Papa and Mama also mentor many of the healers at the Temple, as they both have been healers for a long, long time. People came from near and far to rejuvenate their bodies and spirits, to receive spiritual counseling and spiritual tools to use, and to enjoy meditation and inner journeying where they would easily access more and more of the wholeness of their soul and their soul's long journey through times, places and spaces to be here now, in the beginning years of The New Earth and the 7th Golden Age of Mother Gaia.

It feels wonderful to be home in Sedona. I am looking forward to seeing my friends who I have missed this summer. What an amazing time to be alive here on Gaia! Mother Gaia is without a doubt now once again her beautiful laughing self. I love my life! I love my family. I love all the beauty of Gaia and all the animals and plants and flowers and trees! I love making music and dancing and sharing. I love living in a world that is full of joy!

Onward

There were many quiet circles of pure communion among The Family of Love & Song. There were always new visions both from within each person, created and shared between us, and from the children and young people of our clan. When new babies arrived, all gathered to celebrate, attune and commune with the vastness of this soul who was joining the family; and to welcome him or her with tender and joyful affection in the spirit of wonderment. Each baby transmitted their soul song to be brought forth and also entered in to the hologram for the Akashic record of Gaia.

The possibilities for questing for knowledge from the past and from the future are readily available to all. There is so much to see, so many connections to make, and ever-evolving understandings of the human journey and Gaia's life story sweep the planet. All people have found the profound vastness and truth of who they are and are continuing to evolve personally, collectively, and universally. Through the decades and centuries of the 7th Golden Age, the Family of Love & Song multiplies and expands. The stories, experiences and songs multiply and continue to rise in vibration.

The harmonies quiver with potency and love is the guiding force of all of creation.

How long does this period of harmony, joy and creativity last in the cosmic cycles of time? We are not seeking that far out in to the future. It is more than enough now to be living this new creation here and now. We know the importance of remaining impeccable, and the preciousness of living in harmony and joy. We will share all we perceive and feel of this greater experience of self-realization and universal enlightenment as we progress through this time of the Aquarian Age. Later we will draw out various themes that have played out for this scintillating cycle, and go on to new vistas of creating and sharing, here on Gaia and throughout our Universe and beyond.

The Family of Love & Song will gather in the summers on the porch through it all, knowing and honoring the sacred trust of our particular chalice of love and honoring the wisdom of our ancestors and the miracles of our ever-expanding families. We will continue to celebrate, honor and enjoy the ever unfolding story of love and the fullness of the divine-human.

Triumphant, we are All One!

~August 11, 2012

Saguaro Cactus Flower

in Full Bloom

About the Author

Jewels Maloney is a conscious channel for The Christ-Magdalene energies of healing, inspiration, and love. Jewels has an M.Ed. and Ed.D in Creativity and was a teacher of young children and professor of education for 21 years. She is the author of *Every Child is Holy* - a book for parents and teachers available on Amazon.com, and two books of poetry: *Wadogh: I Am Thankful*, and *Ecstasies and Meditations,* availablc on her website; as well as a variety of articles for professional journals on early childhood education, service learning, and creative teacher education.

Jewels has lived in Sedona, AZ since 2001. She is a Reiki Master and offers Integrated Energy Therapy, Emotional Release, channeled readings, ceremonies in the sacred land and vortex energies of Sedona. Jewels offers Ascension Retreats in Sedona and co-leads Sacred Avalon Journeys to Glastonbury, England and other sacred sites on our beautiful planet.

Visit Jewels at her websites -

www.AscensionIsNow.com

www.AvalonJourney.com

The FeminineChrist.wordpress.com

Suggested Reading

I Remember Union, Flo Aeveia Magdalena

Anna, Grandmother of Jesus, Claire Heartsong

Anna, The Voice of The Magdalenes, Claire Heartsong

The Essene Gospel of Peace, Edmond Bordeaux Szekely (4 books)

The Magdalene Manuscript, Tom Kenyon & Judy Sion

The Gospel of Mary Magdalene, Tau Malachi (and other of his books on the Gnostic Teachings, which have always been an oral tradition).

Kathleen McGowan's series of novels inspired by The Magdalene and The Gnostic traditions: The Expected One, The Book of Love, The Poet Prince.

The Sisterhood of the Dove, Maitreya Zohar

The Power of The Magdalene, Joanna Prentis and Stuart Wilson

The Wisdom of Mary Magdalene (cards), Sharon Hooper

The Woman with the Alabaster Jar, Margaret Starbird

18931192R00096

Made in the USA
Charleston, SC
28 April 2013